MIDCENTURY HOUSES TODAY

THE MONACELLI PRESS

JEFFREY MATZ
LORENZO OTTAVIANI
CRISTINA A. ROSS

MICHAEL BIONDO PHOTOGRAPHY

JOHN MORRIS DIXON INTRODUCTION

NEW CANAAN, CONNECTICUT

MIDCENTURY HOUSES TODAY

For Carolyn French

First published in the United States by The Monacelli Press.

Library of Congress Control Number: 2014940189
ISBN: 9781580933858

Research: Jeffrey Matz
Design: Lorenzo Ottaviani

Printed in China

The Monacelli Press
236 West 27th Street
New York, New York 10001

www.monacellipress.com

Contents

Preface

We hope with this book to share a fascinating journey to the discovery of a group of modern houses located in one of the epicenters of midcentury architecture in America. We are fortunate to live in New Canaan, Connecticut, surrounded by the living history of 91 surviving modern houses.

We selected sixteen houses, covering the period between the1950s and 1978. The houses also represent a range of approaches to preservation and adaptation to contemporary life. Each house is presented with its architect, a timeline of ownership and structural changes, historical photographs, and contemporary photography. This is in part an attempt to unveil the mystery behind the decisions owners have made over time and in part to inspire preservation.

To capture the adaptation and evolution of these modern houses and begin to understand what has been vital to their preservation, we interviewed the owners, builders, architects, and others who have been a part of their transformation. We learned that there is a real passion for living modern among these homeowners. There is a common bond between them that speaks of protection toward these houses. Their perspective seems akin to that of a collector who, with admiration toward a work of art or a precious holding, engages in its stewardship while enjoying its company and all it offers. They cherish their privacy and their independence from the status quo; they understand the history and respect its pedigree. They seek the simplicity and sophistication that is afforded by this style and design, which enables them to live in a comfortably modern lifestyle.

Our interest in these houses is focused not only on their iconic representation of the modern movement in the landscape, but also in their evolution and sometimes their struggle to survive, adapt, and evolve. We are interested in how people live in them today and what modern houses have become as a result.

There is a dynamic process about these modern houses that goes beyond restoration and preservation; it is a continuous journey of discovery. There must be a connection between defining the needs of family living today and understanding the original design intent in order to bring about a restoration or expansion that is meaningful.

—M. B., J. M., L. O., C. A. R.

Then and Now   John Morris Dixon

The history of architecture is one of evolution and adaptation, as new forms emerge in response to cultural, social, and political change. In any era, only a very few structures of exceptional significance can be preserved in their original form or scrupulously restored to it. Most buildings can survive only through adaptation to new circumstances, through alteration to meet new demands.

This circumstance is clearly demonstrated in the town of New Canaan, Connecticut, which became the locus of an extraordinary collection of modern houses in the mid-twentieth century. This group been the subject of many articles and books and the goal for thousands of house-tour participants, but the number of these notable works has dwindled from 118 originally built to 91 today (by one reliable count), and there is mounting concern about their future. This book presents sixteen exemplary survivors, documenting the changes the owners have introduced to extend their lives into the twenty-first century.

These houses could not be adapted to radically new uses—as, for instance, urban commercial buildings can be converted to loft residences or Beaux-Arts mansions to museum or educational use. Their scale, their settings, and the town's zoning regulations require them to remain single-family houses. Nevertheless, to survive, they must meet expectations of contemporary life in terms of space, light, and sustainability.

No property owner would undertake such an updating without a deep appreciation of the aesthetic qualities of the house's design and the ways the architecture enhances daily life. Among owners there is universal admiration for the free flow of their interior spaces, linked through large areas of glass to the natural beauties of their settings.

How modernism reached New Canaan

New Canaan's midcentury houses are heirs to a design movement with roots in the late nineteenth century, a time when advances in the sciences and technology were met with revolutionary concepts in the arts. While this movement was manifested around 1900

God's Acre, New Canaan, Connecticut

in several European cities, its principal center in the United States was Chicago, where protomodern achievements by Louis Sullivan were advanced to a more thorough-going modernism by Frank Lloyd Wright and his followers in the Prairie School.

But the sources of the modernism that emerged in New Canaan are not directly traceable to Midwestern precedents. They reflect instead the design principles promulgated at the Bauhaus school of design in Germany, established in 1919 by the architect Walter Gropius. When the Bauhaus was closed down by the Nazi regime in the 1930s, its key faculty came to the United States and completed the transformation of our architectural profession to modernism. In 1938 Gropius was appointed chairman of the architecture department at the Graduate School of Design at Harvard and was joined there by his young Hungarian colleague, Marcel Breuer. The two also opened an architectural practice together in Cambridge.

The modernism that Gropius and others brought to America had been codified somewhat earlier in the 1932 "Modern Architecture: International Exhibition" at the Museum of Modern Art in New York, which established what came to be called the International Style. To exemplify that style, buildings had to display certain characteristics. They were to be composed of volumes—not masses—that could hover on slim columns or cantilever into space. Conventional windows were replaced with large areas of floor-to-ceiling glass juxtaposed with largely blank walls; roofs were flat (or sometimes very slightly canted). Detail was minimal, devoid of any moldings and other architectural ornament.

The arrival of the modern house in New Canaan was closely linked to the teachings at Harvard, where Gropius and Breuer were passing along their Bauhaus aesthetic to eager American design students. The architects of the town's earliest modern houses were associated with that school and known widely as the Harvard Five. The first to arrive, in 1947, was Eliot Noyes, who was looking for a home in the suburbs for his growing family. Turning 37 that year, Noyes had already had a diversity of experiences as the foundation for his ongoing career. He had worked in Gropius and Breuer's Cambridge office, headed the industrial design department at the Museum of Modern Art—before and after his war years in the Army Air Forces—and had had hands-on exposure to industrial design in the office of Norman Bel Geddes.

While in the service, Noyes had gotten to know fellow airman Thomas J. Watson Jr., soon to become president of IBM. When Noyes started his own firm in New Canaan, he did so with a commission to design typewriters for IBM, the first of several major corporations for which his firm was to provide both architectural and industrial design services. The same year he built his first compact and economical house in New Canaan.

It seems apparent that Noyes helped convince Watson that IBM, whose product line expanded rapidly in the postwar period, could take the lead in the design of both products and buildings. Since most of IBM's expanding facilities were in the suburbs and exurbs north of New York, New Canaan became a likely place for its executives to live, and the modernist design culture that developed in the firm encouraged some of them to build modern houses there.

The town where Noyes settled, and his colleagues would follow, then had a population of about 8,000 (vs. about 19,000 today). It offered the qualities of an archetypal New England town, with white churches facing a green, within a reasonable commute from Manhattan. A branch railroad line terminated in the heart of its appealing downtown, and the Merritt Parkway's convenient link to the city passed through its outer borders. Most important, there was an ample supply of undeveloped land, less expensive than in nearby shoreline communities, much of it too rugged to appeal to developers.

The arrival of Noyes and others needs to be seen in terms of the socioeconomic circumstances of their times. The late 1940s were the first years of the "baby boom," when family formation increased sharply. After more than a decade of suppressed birth

Breuer House 1, Marcel Breuer, 1947

rates due to the Depression and World War II, the future now looked promising, and larger families became the norm. The expanding suburbs were almost universally seen as the proper place for these families to thrive.

The movement of the middle class to the suburbs had been underway for decades and was now accelerated by the proliferation of cars, by highway building, and by federal mortgage guarantees largely denied to older urban areas. Today, when suburban sprawl is widely condemned as too automobile dependent, energy wasting, and socially divisive, it is difficult to realize how committed young professionals of the postwar years were to suburban life.

Gropius and Breuer had conformed to the suburban pattern by building their first U.S. houses in Lincoln, Massachusetts, and other Boston-area modernists built their postwar homes nearby. Until the back-to-the-city movement emerged in the 1960s, young architects saw their suburban houses as emblematic of progress, for themselves and society at large.

Following Noyes to New Canaan

Noyes was one of a group of Harvard Graduate School of Design graduates who were in frequent contact while working in New York earlier in the 1940s. While Noyes was curator of industrial design at MoMA, Philip Johnson was directing the museum's architecture department. John Johansen and Landis Gores were acquainted with Johnson, having studied architecture at Harvard for periods that overlapped with his.

These colleagues of Noyes quickly began to see the merits of living in New Canaan. Preceding them, however, was their teacher at Harvard, Marcel Breuer, who bought land in 1947 and built his first house there a year later. By this time he had left Harvard and the Gropius office to found his own firm in New York, which would produce landmark buildings distributed widely across the United States and the world.

In 1949 Johnson completed his Glass House and its complementary brick-walled guest house, the first of several diverse buildings that would compose his New Canaan compound. Gores, a classmate of Johnson's at Harvard and his partner in architectural practice until 1951, had completed his own relatively grand New Canaan house in 1948. Both Johnson and Gores sought inspiration beyond the limits of their Harvard experience. Johnson looked to the example of Mies van der Rohe, another refugee from the Bauhaus faculty, whose work he had admired since the 1930s; Gores was inspired by the works of Frank Lloyd Wright. And these influences were quite apparent in the houses they designed for themselves.

The fifth member of this initial five was John Johansen. Like Noyes, he had apprenticed in Gropius and Breuer's firm, then had moved on to New York, where he worked at the Skidmore, Owings & Merrill office. By 1951 he had started his own firm in New Canaan and built his family's house there, as compact and unassuming as the first houses of Noyes and Breuer.

Even as these five were settling in New Canaan, their example began attracting other fledgling architects. Victor Christ-Janer, a Yale graduate, became in effect the sixth of the Harvard Five. He built his own house there in 1949, subsequently maintaining his architectural firm there for decades. He was soon followed by John Black Lee, who completed his house in 1952, designed at least seven there for clients, and still lives in the town. Hugh Smallen completed his New Canaan house in 1957 and went on to design several others in the town, at the same time serving as interior and industrial design consultant to a number of corporations. Alan Goldberg arrived in 1966, bringing his experience in office building design to the Noyes office, and within a few years he was directing the firm's architectural practice.

There were frequent social contacts and professional discussions among these architects, all living within a small community. They shared a commitment toward the expansion of the modern movement, which was seen as revolutionizing not just design,

Gores House, Landis Gores, 1948

but also the way people lived—in informally planned houses, closely related to the natural world around them. In all cases, their own houses and those they designed for others filled roles beyond mere shelter, exhibiting their skills and design convictions, setting examples the rest of society was expected to emulate.

First-generation modern houses

A prime design objective for the modern house was efficiency, eliminating little-used spaces and unnecessary room divisions to achieve generous living spaces at reduced cost. In actual practice, the minimal surfaces of modernism, free of moldings and ornament, added to construction cost. Builders could not hide imprecise joints under applied trim, and they instinctively added a premium for features unfamiliar to them. Pressed to produce modern houses with equivalent accommodations to traditional ones, at comparable prices, the pioneering modernist architects had to make them more compact—and persuade clients that they were not getting less for their money.

While a few of the town's modernists had the means to build more lavishly or experimentally (Johnson with his Glass House, for instance), most of the houses they designed were quite modest, with interior floor areas of about 2,000 square feet. Beyond their flat roofs and window walls, these modern houses were distinguished from conventional ones by the freedom with which their spaces were arranged. Several of them had "upside-down" plans, with the bedrooms a floor below the main living spaces; some had the usual bedrooms above, but their entrances were on that upper floor. In a few cases, both sleeping and living spaces were all on a second story, with only some auxiliary spaces, along with covered open areas, at ground level.

With this freedom from accepted space arrangements, modern houses could respond more creatively to the sloping sites many of them occupied. Recessing one side of a lower story into the earth, while the other side was exposed to light and views, was less expensive than locating everything above the ground. Typically, much of the site was left untouched—the contrast of man-made construction to untrammeled nature being a goal of American modernism of the time.

Freedom from traditional conventions also allowed many of these houses to respond more rationally to solar orientation. Many presented extensive full-height glazing—often protected by shading projections—to the south, with fewer and smaller window areas to the north.

While undivided living-dining spaces, with partially partitioned kitchens, were the norm for these houses, bedrooms were enclosed. Children's rooms were often in rows of uniform minimal volumes, a scheme that Frank Lloyd Wright had adopted earlier for many of his houses. Flat roofs facilitated the use of skylights or raised light monitors, rarely if ever seen in premodern houses, to admit daylight to bathrooms and occasionally kitchens, allowing them to be located in central cores, away from exterior walls.

In terms of construction, most of the town's modern houses adopted the established wood-frame system typical of most American houses, as Gropius had done previously. Exposed steel made a rare appearance in the columns of Johnson's Glass House. Exterior walls were typically clad in flush wood boards, vertical or horizontal, painted white or with natural finishes—never the clapboards or shingles characteristic of historical styles and rarely in other paint colors. Flush boards often appeared inside, too, as wall or ceiling surfaces.

In New Canaan, as in much of New England, the house sites typically included fieldstone walls that had once enclosed farm fields, and the modern architects quickly adopted fieldstone for retaining walls and low barriers in their typically minimal landscaping. But the abundant fieldstone soon appeared in exterior walls and inside, as well, in massive fireplaces and their chimneys. These reflected in their bulk and centrality, if not their material, the precedents of local history and the influence of Wright.

Glass House, Philip Johnson, 1949

The one architect in the group who used brick prominently was Philip Johnson. Following the example of Mies van der Rohe, he seemed to favor precisely modular construction materials, and his expertise in the techniques of brickwork is evident in both his houses and the larger structures he was to design later. Note, in his Boissonnas house, how the brick joints in the floors align perfectly with those of the brick piers.

As modern houses began to proliferate in New Canaan, the number of local building contractors familiar with modern architectural details increased. The availability of builders conversant with modern design encouraged construction of more such houses in the town. Further reasons for this clustering in New Canaan were the number of modernist architects at work there and the credibility that the growing number of modern houses lent to the movement in the eyes of potential owners.

New Canaan modernism evolves

While the earliest modern houses in town were modest, larger, more elaborate structures followed. And the austere strictures of Bauhaus design doctrines were further relaxed. Johnson's Boissonnas house (1956) presents a much more complex composition based on square spatial modules, the squares extending out into the treatment of the landscape. Its structural framing rests on massive brick piers, suggesting some kind of archaic precedents. The contemporaneous Villa Ponte by Johansen has a grand layout of four matching pavilions linked by a vaulted main room that spans a stream—the whole scheme clearly inspired by the sixteenth-century villa designs of Andrea Palladio.

Somewhat surprisingly, the New Canaan houses are notable for the frequency, from the start, of symmetrical layouts. These could be interpreted as influenced by the use of symmetry in much of Mies van der Rohe's work—and to sharing Mies's interest in classical precedents. Johnson's Glass House was as unexpected at the time for its rigorous symmetry about both axes as for being entirely enclosed with glass. In Johansen's Campbell house (1951), similarly modest accommodations were housed in symmetrically laid out wings, and there are vestiges of that plan in the asymmetrical Goldberg house (1977) that expanded from its original structure.

The symmetry of Noyes's own second house (1954) is boldly announced by the single central opening in its otherwise solid 80-foot-long front wall of fieldstone. Edward Durell Stone's Celanese house (1959) displays the symmetry characteristic of most of his late buildings, and Gores's Irwin pool house (1960), now the publicly owned Gores Pavilion, has a strictly symmetrical layout throughout. John Black Lee designed a number of New Canaan houses from 1952 to the late 1960s, all compact and economical and most of them emphatically symmetrical.

Response in New Canaan

From the outset, there were many in the town and the surrounding region who welcomed the modern houses and wanted to know them firsthand. The first Modern House Tour took place in 1949, raising about $2,000 for the New Canaan Library building fund. The itinerary included seven recently completed houses: architects' own houses by Breuer, Gores, Johansen, Johnson, and Noyes, plus another house by Breuer and one designed by Breuer with Noyes.

But as more such houses appeared, their architects were considered by many townspeople as disruptive cultural rebels imposing their Ivy League ideas. To some vocal residents, they had "condescended to settle and ruin the landscape with their packing boxes." There was admittedly a certain righteousness among the modernists—in dismissing the reuse of historical styles—that implied condescension. As the divide deepened, a 1952 article in *Holiday* magazine reported that New Canaan had "become an architects' battleground, and everybody talks houses."

Now, more than a half century later, the objections from townspeople have

Lee House 2, John Black Lee 1956

abated, but their house-design preferences have hardly changed. Virtually all the modern houses that have been demolished have made room for replacements in historical revival styles. A few new modern houses have been built in the town over the past decade, most by architects from elsewhere. But it has been decades since the unique spate of modern houses designed by a collegial group of modernists all living right in New Canaan. Today, the town's modern houses are recognized in many ways that help maintain public appreciation of them. The New Canaan Historical Society has accumulated a definitive archive, mounts exhibits, and continues to sponsor well-attended Modern House Day symposiums and tours, biennially in recent years, the latest in 2013. Since Johnson's Glass House was opened as a National Trust property in 2007, its several buildings have been experienced by many thousands of visitors. The National Trust and the local Glass House administration, along with the New Canaan Historical Society and other organizations, have sponsored the New Canaan Mid-Century Modern Houses Survey, which was carried out with state support and published by the Connecticut Commission on Culture and Tourism. The resulting report, published in 2009, lists 91 houses, with descriptions, tables of data, and brief biographies of the architects credited.

Sixteen of the town's modern houses have been entered in the National Register of Historic Places, three between 1997 and 2008, and twelve more as a result of one nomination effort in 2010. National Register houses examined in this book include Breuer house 2, Noyes house 2, Mills house 2, Tatum, and Chivvis. These designations are essentially honorific, however, and the fate of the houses remains dependent on appreciative owners.

Alterations in recent years

Preservation of houses of all kinds has been affected in recent decades by an escalation of what the American middle class expects of a house. Especially in relatively affluent suburbs such as New Canaan, new houses are expected to include such features as media rooms, wine cellars, and generously proportioned ensuite bathrooms for each bedroom. For older houses that are saved, today's energy costs and interior comfort expectations may call for upgrading of glass areas and new state-of-the-art mechanical systems.

Meanwhile, in recent decades the ethos of architectural preservation has been evolving. With the goal of turning back the clock no longer dominant, alteration has come to be seen as not only necessary but also an opportunity to create new aesthetic value through juxtaposition. Additions to midcentury modern buildings do not necessarily harmonize with existing construction. Instead they may introduce a different, more contemporary interpretation of modernism.

Given the current owners' commitment to exceptional design, many of them commissioned contemporary architects of recognized distinction to carry out their updates. There is a certain irony in this, since in the 1950s when modernism first flourished in New Canaan, architects were intent on building anew—on transforming the world aesthetically and socially, with little regard for earlier structures. Additions or alterations to existing structures were considered minor assignments.

The expansion of New Canaan houses—of any period—has long been limited by the town zoning regulations, which restrict ground coverage (rather than, for instance, square footage of usable interior). Since many of the modern houses were one-story rather than a more compact two stories, their ground coverage often left little leeway for expansion, thus making their demolition more likely. In some cases, the addition of a second story was the only permissible option.

Increasing concern over the impact of town zoning on these houses—and wider general respect for their architecture—led to the adoption in 2004 of special provisions for the "Preservation of Modern Houses." The special protection for modern work did not originate in isolation, but as part of a movement to protect any property seen as historic. With the approval of a special permit, requirements such as minimum side yard dimensions can be reduced or maximum building coverage exceeded.

For a modern house to qualify for a special permit, it must be recognized as "worthy of continued preservation" by the New Canaan Historical Society or "other source acceptable" to the town. An authoritative source must also verify that "the proposed improvement shall retain the architectural integrity" of the house. This permit remains in effect only so long as the house "is preserved and maintained as the principal structure on the property." While few houses have so far benefited from this provision, it offers improved chances for the survival—and complementary alterations—of other houses.

The Gores Pavilion illustrates an unusual instance of adaptation through public, rather than private, action. Built in 1957 as a pool house for a larger residence, the building became town property in 2006, when the estate on which it stood was acquired as public parkland. The town's initial intention to demolish it was reversed through the efforts of local preservation groups. With private funding for repairs and modest alterations, the building now accommodates events and exhibitions as an outpost of the New Canaan Historical Society.

The houses chosen for this book testify to the value now placed on midcentury modern architecture. And they illustrate the various strategies for adapting them to twenty-first-century expectations. Their examples encourage extending the useful lives of existing structures of all kinds, a key aspect of today's sustainability ethic. And the success with which they have been updated increases the general appreciation of such houses, worldwide, demonstrating what they can offer today as inspiring environments for living.

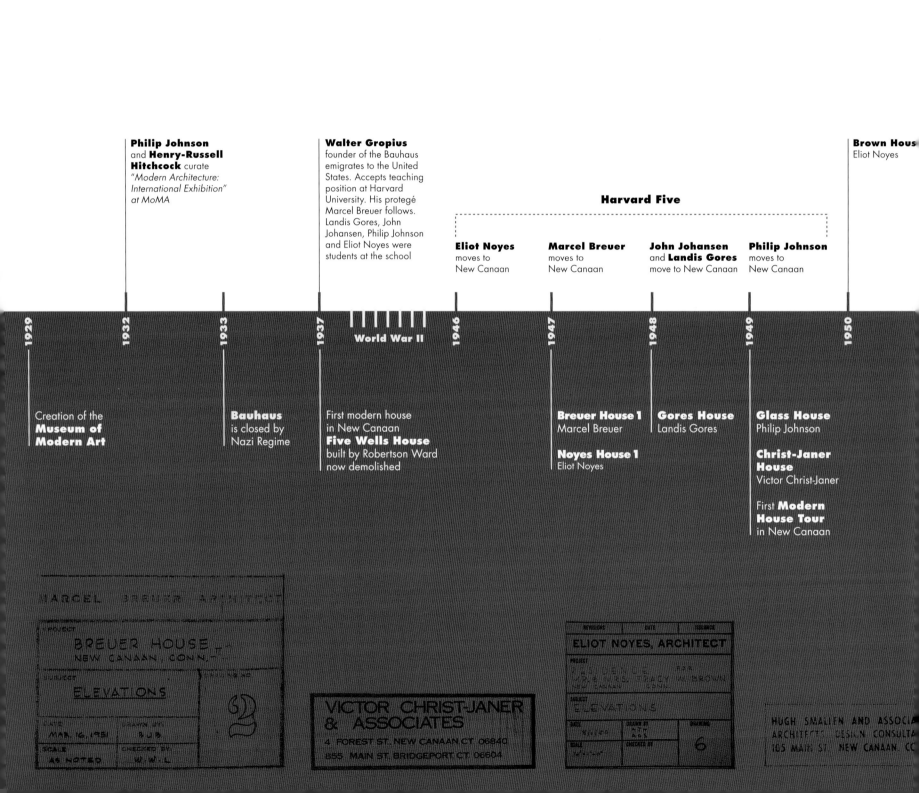

Philip Johnson and **Henry-Russell Hitchcock** curate *"Modern Architecture: International Exhibition"* at MoMA

Walter Gropius founder of the Bauhaus emigrates to the United States. Accepts teaching position at Harvard University. His protegé Marcel Breuer follows. Landis Gores, John Johansen, Philip Johnson and Eliot Noyes were students at the school

Brown Hous Eliot Noyes

Harvard Five

Eliot Noyes moves to New Canaan

Marcel Breuer moves to New Canaan

John Johansen and **Landis Gores** move to New Canaan

Philip Johnson moves to New Canaan

1929

1932

1933

1937

World War II

1946

1947

1948

1949

1950

Creation of the **Museum of Modern Art**

Bauhaus is closed by Nazi Regime

First modern house in New Canaan **Five Wells House** built by Robertson Ward now demolished

Breuer House 1 Marcel Breuer

Noyes House 1 Eliot Noyes

Gores House Landis Gores

Glass House Philip Johnson

Christ-Janer House Victor Christ-Janer

First **Modern House Tour** in New Canaan

MARCEL BREUER ARCHITECT

PROJECT
BREUER HOUSE
NEW CANAAN, CONN.

SUBJECT
ELEVATIONS

DATE MAR. 16, 1951 DRAWN BY BJB
SCALE AS NOTED CHECKED BY W.W.L

VICTOR CHRIST-JANER & ASSOCIATES
4 FOREST ST. NEW CANAAN, CT. 06840
855 MAIN ST. BRIDGEPORT, CT. 06604

REVISIONS DATE ISSUANCE
ELIOT NOYES, ARCHITECT
PROJECT
RESIDENCE FOR
MR. & MRS. TRACY M. BROWN
NEW CANAAN CONN.
SUBJECT
ELEVATIONS
DATE DRAWN BY DRAWING
SCALE CHECKED BY 6

HUGH SMALLEN AND ASSOCIA
ARCHITECTS DESIGN CONSULTA
105 MAIN ST. NEW CANAAN, CC

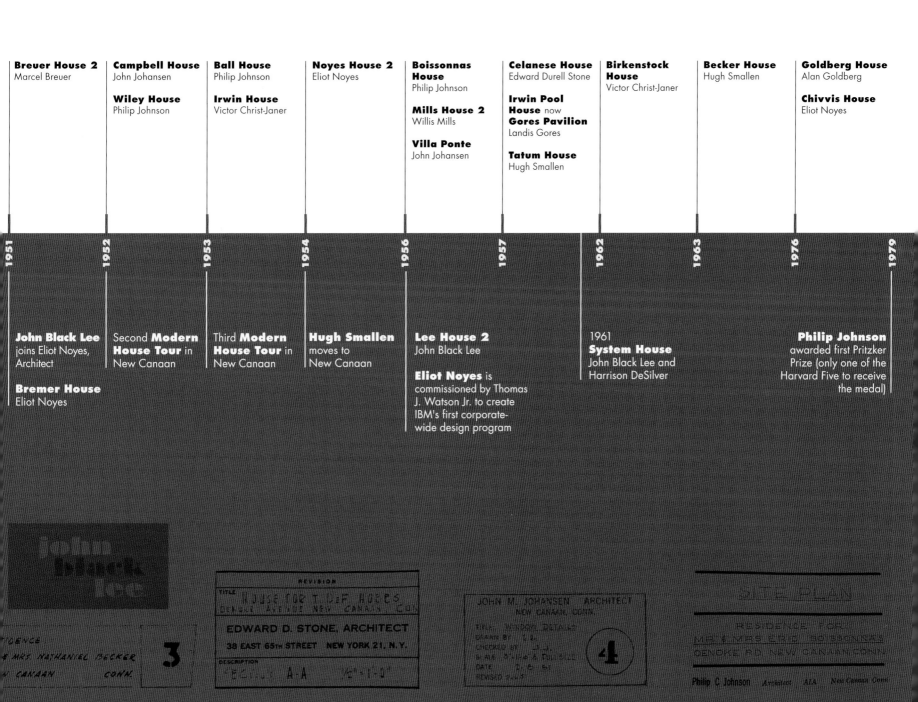

Breuer House 2
Marcel Breuer

Campbell House
John Johansen

Wiley House
Philip Johnson

Ball House
Philip Johnson

Irwin House
Victor Christ-Janer

Noyes House 2
Eliot Noyes

Boissonnas House
Philip Johnson

Mills House 2
Willis Mills

Villa Ponte
John Johansen

Celanese House
Edward Durell Stone

Irwin Pool House now **Gores Pavilion**
Landis Gores

Tatum House
Hugh Smallen

Birkenstock House
Victor Christ-Janer

Becker House
Hugh Smallen

Goldberg House
Alan Goldberg

Chivvis House
Eliot Noyes

1951 **1952** **1953** **1954** **1956** **1957** **1962** **1963** **1976** **1979**

John Black Lee joins Eliot Noyes, Architect

Bremer House
Eliot Noyes

Second **Modern House Tour** in New Canaan

Third **Modern House Tour** in New Canaan

Hugh Smallen moves to New Canaan

Lee House 2
John Black Lee

Eliot Noyes is commissioned by Thomas J. Watson Jr. to create IBM's first corporate-wide design program

1961
System House
John Black Lee and Harrison DeSilver

Philip Johnson awarded first Pritzker Prize (only one of the Harvard Five to receive the medal)

REVISION
TITLE HOUSE FOR T. DeF. HOLES
DENORE AVENUE NEW CANAAN CON
EDWARD D. STONE, ARCHITECT
38 EAST 65TH STREET NEW YORK 21, N.Y.
DESCRIPTION
SECTION A-A 1/8"=1'-0"

3

IDENCE
& MRS. NATHANIEL BECKER
CANAAN CONN.

JOHN M. JOHANSEN ARCHITECT
NEW CANAAN, CONN.
TITLE WINDOW DETAILS
DRAWN BY J.J.
CHECKED BY J.J.
SCALE 3"=1'-0 & FULL SIZE
DATE 7-15-54
REVISED 24H3

4

SITE PLAN
RESIDENCE FOR
MR. & MRS. ERIC BOISSONNAS
OENOKE RD. NEW CANAAN CONN.
Philip C Johnson Architect AIA New Canaan Conn.

1951
Breuer House 2
Marcel Breuer architect

1975–76
Owner 2
Renovation and addition, garage
Herbert Beckhard architect

1980–82
Pool house, attached greenhouse
Herbert Beckhard architect

1990
Owner 3

1997
Owner 4

2004
Owner 5
Owner 6

2005–7
Construction main house, addition, pool house
Toshiko Mori architect

Breuer House 2 1951 Marcel Breuer

A building will last for many years, for several generations. Changes are just as much a part of it as its rigid, everlasting structure. Neither one-sided oversimplification nor turned-down compromise offers solution. The search for a definite, clear answer that satisfies opposite aims and needs is what takes, architecture out of the realm of abstraction and gives it life and art.

—Marcel Breuer

Marcel Breuer built his second family home in New Canaan in 1951, and he lived there for twenty-four years with his wife and two children. The house was modest, a single story with three bedrooms and two baths, on four acres of land.

A fieldstone facade faced the road, creating an understated presence. The shallow U-shaped plan enclosing the entrance courtyard was as functional and rational as the volume. Living spaces and the master bedroom were at one end, service spaces in the center, and children's and guest bedrooms at the other end of the house. The interior was painted in neutral shades with accent walls of primary colors. As with many other Breuer designs, fieldstone was the primary building material, with glazing dominating the rear facade, which opened the house to the landscape.

When the house was sold in 1975, the new owners retained Breuer's firm to expand and renovate it. Herbert Beckhard, one of the partners, became the project architect for a new bedroom wing, a pool and pool house, and a greenhouse.

After 1990 the house changed hands several times, with work done each time to update it, until a developer purchased it in 2004 with plans to raze it. The New Canaan Historical Society made it their mission to bring attention to the house and change its fate during the Modern House Tour in the fall of 2004. A couple on the tour purchased the property and saved it from demolition.

The house had deteriorated over time, and it needed more attention than the buyers originally anticipated. The search for an architect led them to a lecture on mid-century modern houses by Toshiko Mori. Following this impromptu meeting, a conversation began about moderns and their vision for preservation and expansion. "We were taken with the thought that perhaps we could save an important modern house," one of the owners explained. "The goal was to remain true to Breuer's original concept, while increasing the square footage of the house and updating its infrastructure."

Mori envisioned the restoration of the

original house and the addition of a new two-story wing with a glazed connection between the two. Early in the process it was clear that the structure was unsound. The house was taken down and rebuilt with the same stones (they had been carefully numbered) and all of the details re-created. The interior walls were removed, creating an open area, which included the living room, dining room, and kitchen. Breuer's original fireplace remains the heart of the house, centered on the living room wall and anchoring the space. Mori designed new cabinetry and introduced a neutral palette of white, gray, and brown. To raise the ceiling height in the main living areas and increase natural light, she designed a clerestory, carefully set back on the roof to preserve the original Breuer street facade.

The new wing, with a glass curtain wall, replaced the masonry Beckhard wing, using the same footprint but extending to two stories. Family bedrooms were moved to the addition and connected to the main house with a staircase also

Original floor plan

1 Foyer
2 Living room
3 Dining room
4 Kitchen
5 Bedroom
6 Bathroom
7 Storage
8 Courtyard
9 Patio

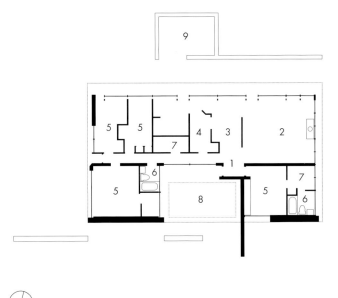

enclosed in glass. Curtain walls of milk-white translucent glass admit natural light while protecting the privacy of the occupants. The second story projects beyond the first, creating the illusion of being suspended in flight, hovering just at the level of the treetops. The use of glass on the rear facade creates a translucency that blurs the lines between indoor and outdoor spaces. The views from within the house toward the surrounding landscape and structures are inviting and alluring. "The relationship between the existing house and the addition expresses the contrast between heavy and light in both material and form," Mori explained. "While the original structure is composed primarily of heavy stone walls and large expanses of glass, the addition proposes a material palette of finer gradation and more innovative application."

The approach to the house is now more refined and direct. The front facade of the original house stands proud, unchanged, but Mori's design incorporates the landscape to create a new sense of arrival.

Current floor plan

1 Foyer
2 Living room
3 Dining room
4 Kitchen
5 Bedroom
6 Bathroom
7 Storage
8 Courtyard
9 Terrace
10 Family room
11 Study
12 Garage
13 Pantry
14 Butler's pantry

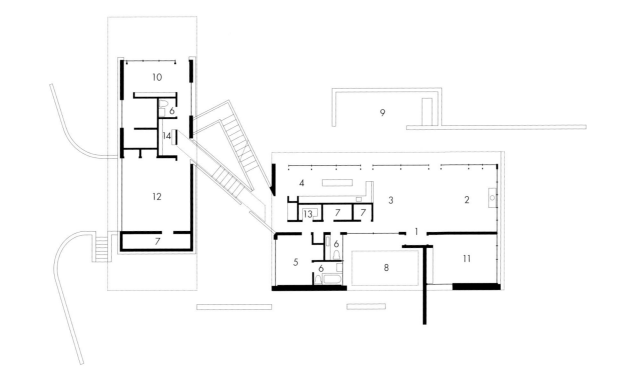

Site plan

1 Main house
2 New wing
3 Pool
4 Pool house
5 Rooftop greenhouse
6 Driveway

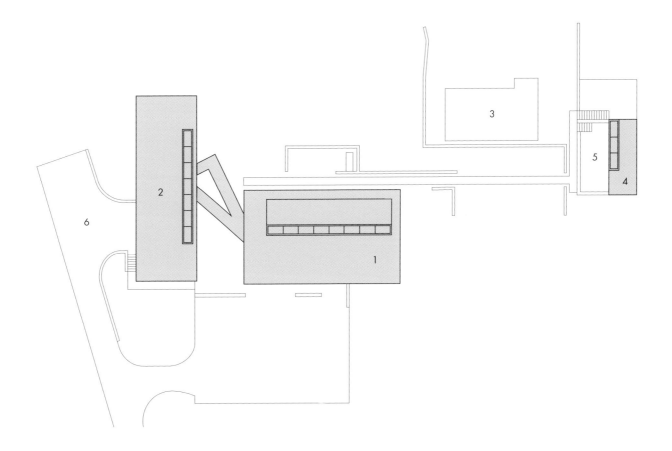

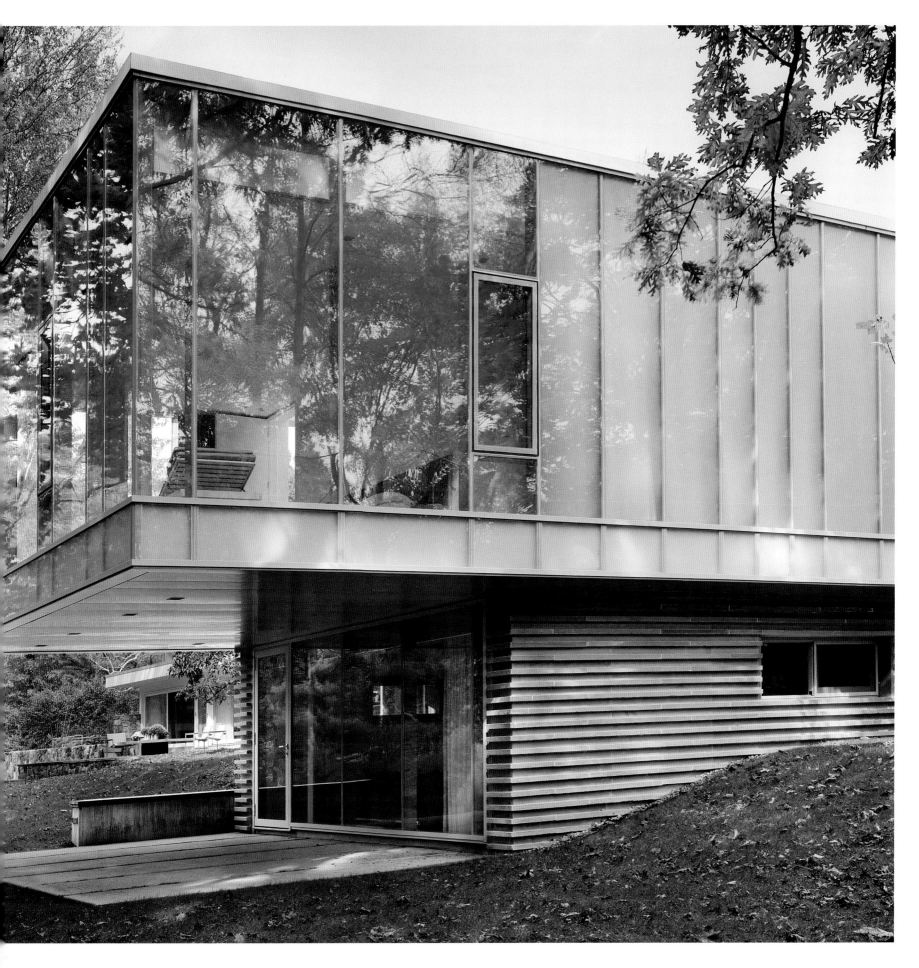

1954	**1964**	**1976**	**1977**
Noyes House 2	Storage shed	Studio	Interior modification
Eliot Noyes architect	Eliot Noyes architect	Eliot Noyes architect	master bedroom

Noyes House 2 1954 Eliot Noyes

It is no coincidence that an architect often expresses himself most clearly in a house designed for himself and his family. As an architect, he will have thought a lot about how people could live as opposed to how they do and how by architectural means he could expand the scope and richness of life within the house.

—Eliot Noyes

Eliot Noyes was the first modernist architect to settle in New Canaan, and his original house, known as the Tallman house, was one of the first modernist designs to be built there. He and his wife, Molly, discovered the community in 1946 during a search for a place close to New York to raise their family. The combination of affordable land and relatively unrestricted zoning persuaded the couple to choose New Canaan.

Trained at the Harvard Graduate School of Design and in the offices of Walter Gropius and Marcel Breuer, Noyes served as the first curator of industrial design at the Museum of Modern Art, working under Philip Johnson. He convinced his mentors Breuer and Johnson as well as his colleague Landis Gores to join him in New Canaan. The group, with the addition of John Johansen, became known as the Harvard Five. Other modernist architects, including Victor Christ-Janer, soon followed.

In 1954, having outgrown the Tallman House, Noyes built his second family residence in New Canaan. Sited in a grove of trees on a naturally wooded six-acre parcel, the house is a simple, one-story building with fieldstone walls and wood cladding that blends easily into the landscape. A 101-foot-long fieldstone and masonry wall protects the entrance facade from view. The house itself is a composition of two parallel rectangular wings, one for living space and the other for private areas, with a courtyard between them. The flat roof overhangs the exterior walls on all sides, creating sheltered outdoor circulation. The main entrance is centered on the courtyard; a pair of large solid wood sliding barn doors welcomes visitors. The entrance is mirrored on the opposite end of the courtyard by a matching portal. The courtyard is open to the sky at its center, creating a dramatic spatial composition.

The long sides of both wings are glazed, a striking contrast to the monumentality of the perpendicular fieldstone walls. The glass walls allow an uninterrupted visual connection from the woods through the living space, the courtyard, the private areas, and out to the woods again on the opposite side.

The open plan of the public wing accommodates the foyer, the kitchen, the living and dining space with a freestanding fireplace, and a study beyond, which Noyes used as a home office. The private wing is partitioned as five bedrooms and two baths, with a small area that serves as both a foyer and a second study.

There is no distinction between interior and exterior materials. Fieldstone walls and slate floors blur the boundaries between inside and out, while the expanses of glass offer views that juxtapose interior and exterior spaces with the landscape.

The facade of the bedroom wing is made up of a black-painted steel-frame window system divided into a grid of eight modules per bedroom. Two panels extend from the floor to sill height; two double-height panels function as sliding windows, with two additional panels rising to the ceiling. In the public wing full floor-to-ceiling sliding doors on both sides open to the courtyard and the landscape.

Original floor plan

1 Foyer
2 Living room
3 Dining room
4 Kitchen
5 Bedrom
6 Bathroom
7 Study
8 Patio courtyard
9 Terrace
10 Storage

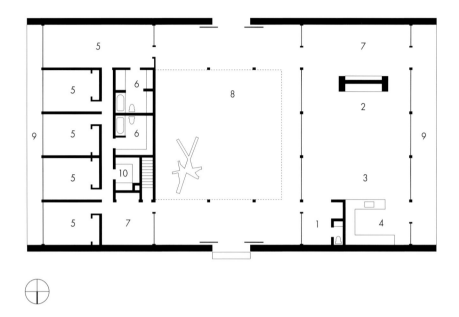

The house as it stands now is a time capsule, with the interiors preserved as they were when Eliot and Molly Noyes lived there with their family. All of the furniture and works of art were acquired over time, objects that spoke to both of them of good design. Included are works by Charles and Ray Eames, Alexander Calder, Jacques Lipchitz, Picasso, Miro, and Matisse, as well as an antique carousel horse and maquettes of sculptures. For Noyes, art was an essential part of life: "This intimate and inescapable blending of art and life enriches our daily existence. My conclusion is that modern architecture is good for art collections—it provides good surfaces, good and varied lighting, interesting textures and backgrounds. Beyond all this, it provides an intimate, normal, and unselfconscious exposure to works of art, which enables us to enjoy them to the fullest." The family commissioned several works by Calder, including the stabile *The Black Beast* (1957), which was installed in the courtyard. *Snow Flurry* (1950), a low-hanging mobile was acquired for the living room, and a second *Untitled* (1957) was selected for another area of the room to balance the space.

The property is still owned by the Noyes family, which is committed to its preservation.

Current floor plan

1 Foyer
2 Living room
3 Dining room
4 Kitchen
5 Bedrom
6 Bathroom
7 Study
8 Patio courtyard
9 Terrace
10 Storage

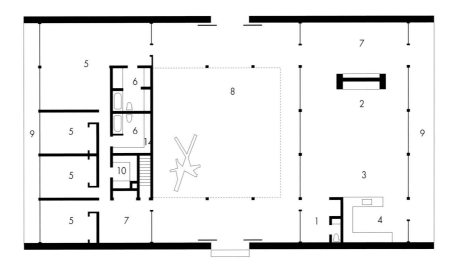

Site plan

1 Main house
2 Studio
3 Driveway
4 Courtyard
5 Shed

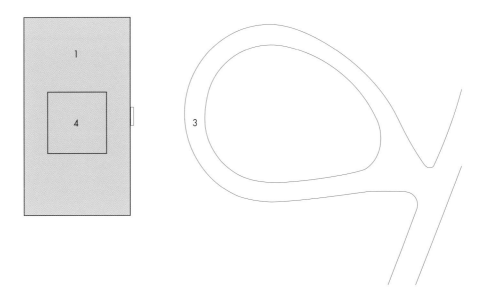

1952
Wiley House
Philip Johnson architect

1960
Alteration barn

1978
Owner 2

1994
Owner 3

2002
Additions unbuilt
Philip Johnson architect

2008
Additions, pool house,
landscaping
Roger Ferris architect

Wiley House 1952 Philip Johnson

*All architecture is shelter, all
great architecture is the design
of space that contains, cuddles,
exalts, or stimulates the persons
in that space.*

—Philip Johnson

Robert C. Wiley, a developer with ambitions of building modern houses, commissioned Philip Johnson to design one for his family. Johnson chose the site, just over six acres, with an old barn on the property. The character of the landscape was akin to that of the Glass House, with a steep drop in grade, stone walls, and majestic trees.

For Johnson, the Wiley house was an extension of the design principle of the Glass House: transparency for public space juxtaposed with a solid enclosure for the private areas. From the road, the glass cube appears to float on a shallow podium. In fact, the podium is built into the slope, and an interior stair connects to the family spaces below.

Johnson called this cube the "glass prism," and he set it at a 180-degree angle to the podium. Within the cube are the main entrance, the living/dining room, and the kitchen. A freestanding circular fireplace is a focal point of the living space. The slate floor extends onto the roof of the podium, providing terraces on two sides of the cube. The podium houses

four bedrooms and a sitting room, all of which have unobstructed views of the larger landscape and access to the lawn immediately outside.

While the basic concept of transparency versus opacity is applied here and at the Glass House, Johnson explained that the experience of the space is very different: "The effect from inside—quite the opposite of my Glass House—is that of a cage."

The vertical members on the glass facade frame a view of the barn set in a grove of hickory trees that is particularly dramatic at night. During the day awnings shade the interior.

At a respectful distance from the house, Johnson placed a circular pool near the barn and connected the complex of buildings with a rectangular walkway.

As Richard Foster, a partner of Johnson's, observed, "The blend of forms and the sensitive use of materials are both original and successful. The wood detailing of the windows was very carefully crafted and formed an important element of design."

After 1960 the house changed hands several times, and it stood vacant for a number of years before the current owner acquired the property in 1994. An art collector, he commissioned Johnson to design a gallery on the property, but the project was not built. The house originally had five bedrooms, but one is now used as a family/sitting room.

Working with architect Roger Ferris, the current owner has completed an extensive restoration of the main house and added new elements and enclosures to the property. The barn, once converted into a pool house, has been restored and expanded as the art gallery the owner envisioned. Ferris designed a new pool house, which is built into the landscape and hidden by a rubblestone wall that encloses a courtyard for the pool area.

According to Ferris, "This project expands the program of the original modern residence by Philip Johnson, to integrate new structures into the spectacular setting of the house with a design rooted in a respectful contextual response. The new

Original floor plan

1 Foyer
2 Living room
3 Dining room
4 Kitchen
5 Bedroom
6 Bathroom
7 Storage
8 Patio/Terrace

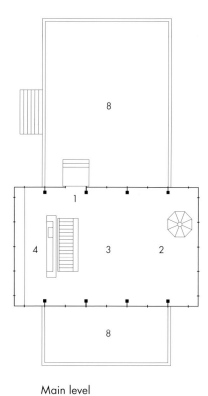

Main level

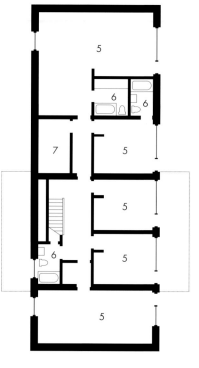

Lower level

art gallery, pool house, and garage re-inforce the architectural clarity of the original glass house. The art gallery, a reconstructed nineteenth-century barn, offers a solid black contemporary counterpoint to Johnson's transparent house. The pool house and the garage are both set into the hillside with a single exposed wall revealing the plinth of the original house."

Current floor plan

1 Foyer
2 Living room
3 Dining room
4 Kitchen
5 Bedroom
6 Bathroom
7 Storage
8 Patio/Terrace
9 Family room

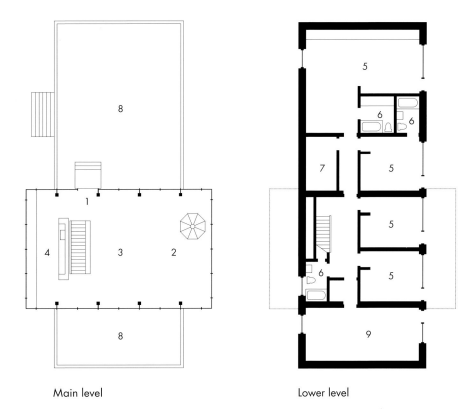

Main level   Lower level

Site plan

1 Main house
2 Garage
3 Pool house
4 Pool
5 Barn
6 Driveway

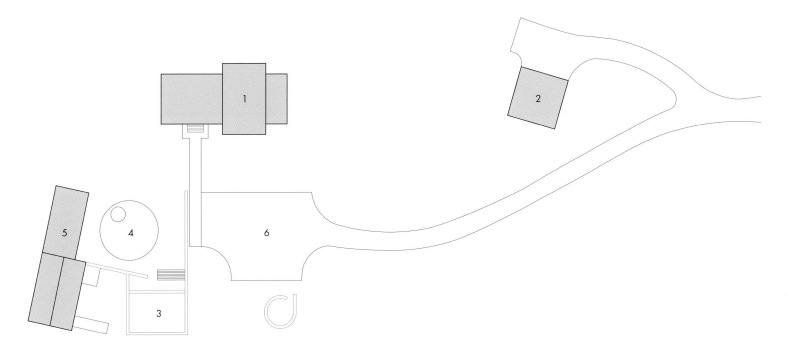

1953
Irwin House
Victor Christ-Janer architect

1961
Owner 2

1964
Addition bathroom
Victor Christ-Janer architect

1972
Fire reconstruction
Victor Christ-Janer architect

1973
Owner 3

1976–78
Renovation studio
alterations porch, balconies
Silvia F. Erskine Associates

1984
Swimming
pool

1999
Owner 4

2013
Restoration
main house
and kitchen
by owner

Irwin House 1953 Victor Christ-Janer

The modern movement brought with it a philosophy of space and proportions different from the colonial clapboard house, but not so very different in essence. Both styles grow from integrity in the use of materials and construction methods.

—Victor Christ-Janer

The Irwin house is one of two speculative houses Victor Christ-Janer designed in New Canaan in collaboration with the builder Robert Roles. In 1954 William A. Irwin and his wife purchased this one, which continues to bear their name.

The house is sited high on a hill in dense woods, with views of a ponded area of the Noroton River. The property abuts a bird sanctuary, which provided a level of privacy that allowed the east facade to be composed entirely of large spans of glass. In contrast, the north and south facades are solid, open only at the entrances at the center.

The two-story house presents as a cantilevered structure set on a plinth. The upper level is clad in vertical wood siding while the plinth is stucco. On the east facade, a deep, cantilevered overhang encloses a balcony running the length of the house, offering both protection from direct sun and wide views of the woods, the ponds, and the sunrises. The north and south facades are identical, with steps leading up to glazed doors and windows

sheltered by shallow projections above. The west side of the house is nested into the hillside. The garage is precisely sited at a 45-degree angle to the house.

In plan, the house was configured on a grid of nine squares. Partitions define three identical bedrooms on the west side. In the center with the service core, the grid is less apparent, while the living and dining space on the east remains open. A freestanding, two-sided fireplace informally allocates the space as one-third for dining and two-thirds for living area. In the foyer, opposite the front door, stairs descend to the lower level, an open unobstructed space similar to the living/dining area above. Originally this level was not finished, but its potential as a space for additional bedrooms or a play area for children was noted from the beginning.

The Irwins sold the property in 1961. In 1972 the house was badly damaged by fire, but it was rebuilt according to the original plans. Christ-Janer added a second story to the garage in 1987, converting it into a study/guest house.

The addition echoes the cantilevered structure of the main house.

Restoration and renovation projects by the present owners have opened the house still further and addressed thermal performance. Solid wood exterior doors were replaced with insulated wood-framed glass doors to extend the transparency of the glass walls. Steps leading to the entrances were widened to center and align the glass openings to the house along north-south axis. These two points of entry bookend a long corridor, and the new glass doors have transformed it into a light-filled space that is visually connected to the landscape. On the exterior, the entrance sequence has been reversed so that the approach to the house is from a courtyard area on the north side. Once the entrance was moved, the wall between the foyer and the kitchen was removed to expand the kitchen with a breakfast area in front of the original glazed opening.

The owners' commitment to the integrity of the architecture is seen in the custom

Original floor plan

1 Foyer
2 Living room
3 Dining room
4 Kitchen
5 Bedroom
6 Bathroom
7 Back entrance
8 Balcony

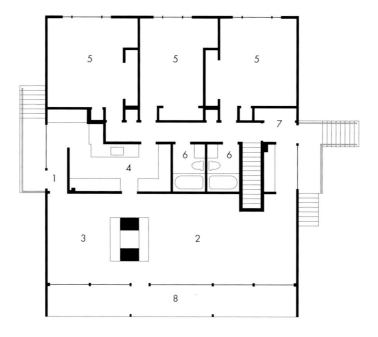

millwork and meticulous restoration that has preserved the character and original design intent while carefully upgrading the interior with changes that enhance the original detailing of trim, door styles, and flooring throughout. The living room and dining room were originally designed with paneled wood walls and acoustical tile ceilings. These surfaces are now white-painted sheetrock, updating the aesthetic and bringing more reflective light into the spaces. Works from the owners' extensive art collection rotate with the seasons to complement the views, and their art glass collection, displayed throughout the house, responds to the reflection of light penetrating the spaces.

Current floor plan

1 Foyer
2 Living room
3 Dining room
4 Kitchen
5 Bedroom
6 Bathroom
7 Back entrance
8 Balcony
9 Breakfast room
10 Study

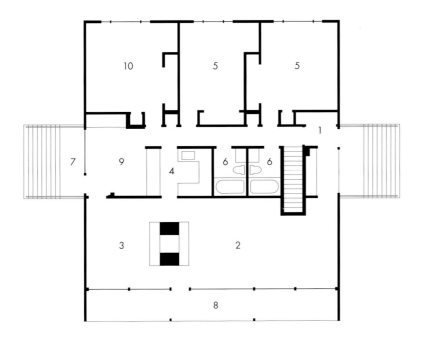

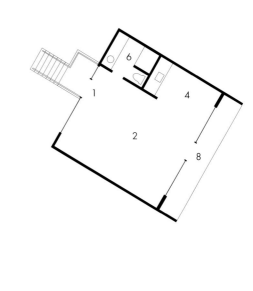

Site plan

1 Main house
2 Guesthouse
3 Storage
4 Driveway
5 Pool

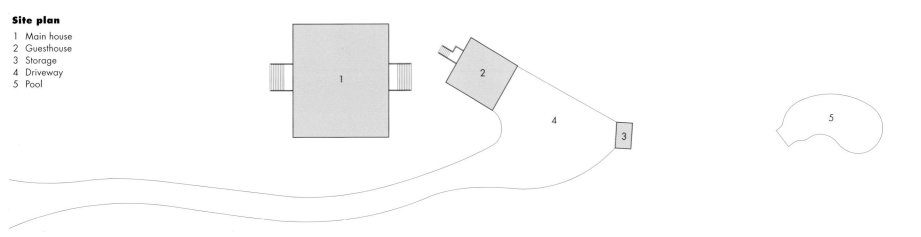

1953		1962			1977	2005	2007
Ball House		Addition garage, guesthouse			Owner 5	Owner 6	Restoration main house,
Philip Johnson architect	1960	Philip Johnson architect ·	1965	1969	Renovation guesthouse	Restoration courtyard	guesthouse, garage
	Owner 2		Owner 3	Owner 4	Philip Johnson architect	Cristina A. Ross architect	Cristina A. Ross architect

Ball House 1953 Philip Johnson

Architecture is surely not the design of space, certainly not the massing or organization of volumes. These are auxiliary to the main point, which is the organization of procession. Architecture exists only in time.

—Philip Johnson

Little is known about Alice Ball, who commissioned Philip Johnson to design this house on a 2.2-acre site. Occupying only 1,500 square feet, the house has remained virtually unchanged for more than sixty years. Johnson's design concept was deeply influenced by a Miesian vocabulary: a composition of horizontal planes with an asymmetrical entrance and based on voids and solids executed in glass and masonry.

Identical entrances on the front and back are marked by deep patios extending out from the inside of the house, carrying the same slate as the interior flooring of the house itself. Transparency blurs the line between what is indoors and what is outdoors as they visually converge into a single space. The cross-axial movement starts at the front entrance, continues through the house and out toward a gravel courtyard in the center of the property, and extends out to the landscape beyond. The gravel courtyard is surrounded on three sides by a low stone wall, with an opening in the center

allowing access into the woods.

On the front of the house, to the south of the entrance, a 100-foot-long wall seems to stand guard, as it anchors and frames the house on the site. In 1962 when Johnson designed a guesthouse/garage, the wall was extended to create an enclosed courtyard, a secret garden that connects the two buildings.

The plan of the main house is simple: a generous multipurpose space serves as living room, dining room, and foyer with the central kitchen between it and the two bedrooms and baths. Ten-foot-high ceilings and glass walls make the space feel grander, as does the floating cabinetry separating the main area from the kitchen, a strategy for spatial separation also seen in the Glass House. There are no windows, just curtain walls of glass; a twenty-two-foot skylight over the kitchen admits natural light and connects the house to the sky.

Johnson introduced the concept of the floating fireplace in this house. It stands almost two feet above the floor and proj-

ects about ten inches forward from the wall, completely surrounded by a Vermont soapstone surround and mantel. The jet-black color was obtained through a mineral oiling process, which further deepens the color and richness of the stone. The rectilinear and minimalist design makes the fireplace seem as if it were a suspended sculpture.

Soon after its completion, the Ball house became known as "The Pink Palace," a reference to its exterior cladding of thick, trowelled smooth salmon-on-pink colored stucco, which originally had a magnificent shimmer from glass additives. Johnson called it "the little jewel box," and by all accounts it was just that.

The current owner is an architect who considers herself a steward of its preservation. Johnson's plans and the construction records from the Murphy Brinkworth Construction Company have guided the restoration process. At the urging of Johnson and other architects, Murphy Brinkworth, contractor for the Seagram Building and other prestigious

Original floor plan

1 Foyer
2 Living room
3 Dining room
4 Kitchen
5 Bedroom
6 Bathroom
7 Courtyard

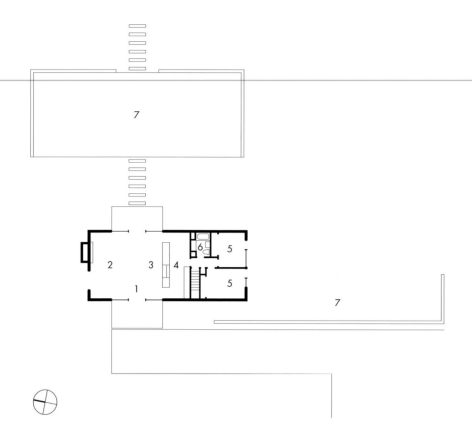

projects in New York, opened a satellite office in New Canaan, assuring the same level of construction quality for their Connecticut work.

Today it is impossible to replicate the quality of the original stucco color and finish of the Ball house, but the interior finishes and details have been restored. Renovations often reveal details of construction and design that would otherwise remain concealed. Here Johnson introduced a number of ingenious details that were advanced for this period. Lightweight concrete-encased steel beams frame the floor of the house; construction fabric was laid between the beams in two directions and reinforced with handmade wire mesh and rebar. The concrete was poured and allowed to set, and later covered with an overlay of Vermont slate as the finish surface. While other houses were framed in wood and constrained by the skills of the local labor available, Johnson continued to design and build in steel, glass, and masonry as he did for large-scale projects in New York. Specifications for materials, fixtures, and hardware were identical to those of the Seagram Building and the Glass House.

Current floor plan

1 Foyer
2 Living room
3 Dining room
4 Kitchen
5 Bedroom
6 Bathroom
7 Courtyard
8 Garage

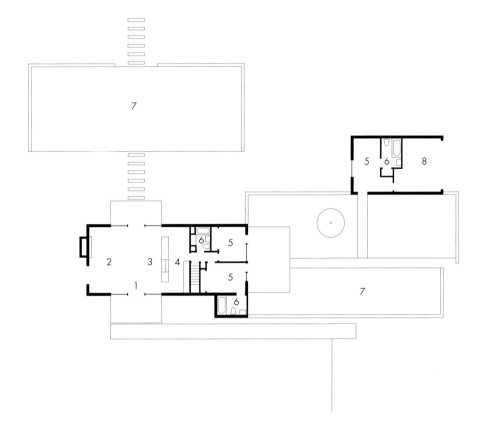

Site plan

1 Main house
2 Guesthouse
3 Courtyard
4 Driveway

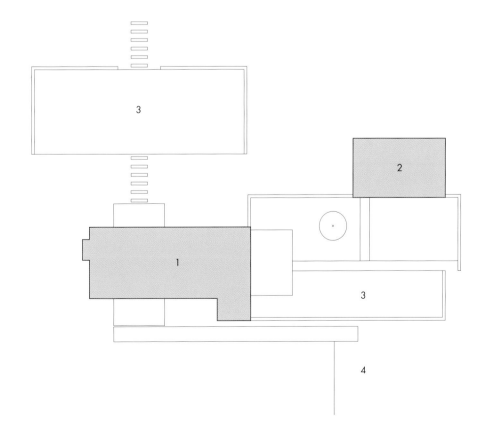

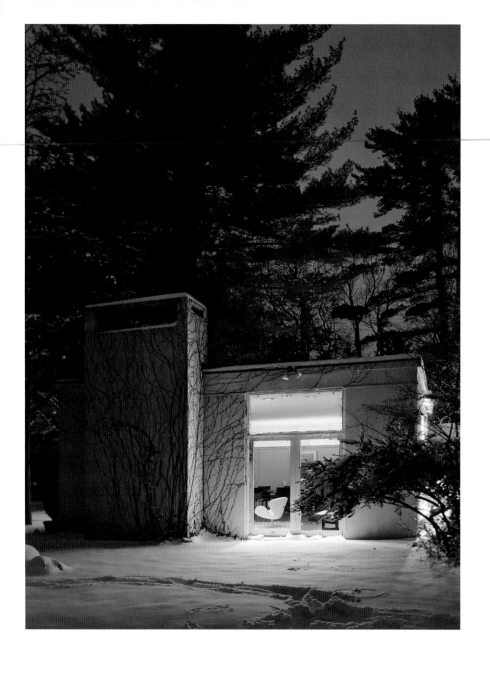

1950
Brown House
Eliot Noyes architect

1960
Pool, pool house,
guesthouse

1980
Owner 2

1998
Owner 3

2002
Partial demolition, new construction,
and second-story addition
Joeb Moore architect

2004
Owner 4

2005
Renovation pool, pool house,
and guesthouse
Amanda Martocchio architect

Brown House 1950 Eliot Noyes

*Details must play their part in relation
to the overall concept and character
of the building, and are the means
by which the architect may underline
his main idea, reinforce it, echo it,
intensify or dramatize it.*

—Eliot Noyes

For this house, commissioned by Tracy W. Brown, Eliot Noyes developed a design based on efficiency, simplicity, and transparency, alluding to the Bauhaus principle of form follows function. It was a sophisticated approach to making spaces functional by creating order, while minimizing partitions in the public areas and eliminating all ornamentation. Natural materials, such as stone and wood, add warmth while expanses of glass define the proportions of the spaces.

On approach, the house originally presented as a one-story structure framed by mature trees and gardens. Within, the foyer extended through the space to a balcony that framed views over the landscape. A stair descended to the formal and entertaining areas on the lower level. These spaces opened out to the lawn through glass walls and doors that invited the outside in. Bedrooms and family spaces were on the main level, reversing the typical residential stacking.

In 1962 Noyes designed a pool and pool house on the flat lawn behind the house.

The Browns listed the house for sale in 1980, noting in the prospectus, "No barriers are presented to Noyes's unique structure where Nature and home are one." The house had a subsequent owner, and in 1998 was sold to a builder as his personal residence.

The builder/owner explained, "Our desire to buy the house emerged from the stunning presentation of the property with fields of pachysandra, the amenities of a relatively new pool house/guest house with two bedrooms, and the open-plan layout of the house, which we had not experienced before." He and his wife planned to live in the house and expand it over time, but it soon became apparent that the house needed more immediate attention. With Joeb Moore as their architect, the couple embarked on a journey of discovery.

Constrained by zoning regulations that limited the expansion of the footprint, the architect realized that the only option was to add a second story. In part due to the topography of the site, the front would

be viewed as having a second story and the back as having a third story, of which the lower level would remain as a walk out onto the landscape. The bedrooms, with the exception of a guest room, were moved to the addition, allowing the main level to become living space.

The first and lower levels were rebuilt and refurbished, retaining the openness in the interior. The living room, dining room, and kitchen, originally on the lower level, were all relocated. The lower level now accommodates a family room and guest room as well as service and storage areas.

Acknowledging Noyes's original design, the architect inserted a reveal between the first and second floors of the house that created a reference point and marked the joint between historical and new. The original stair was relocated and replaced by an open floating stair connecting all three levels. The stair articulates a vertical connection between the past and the present, a connection that can be seen through the front facade as a sculptural element. These interventions created

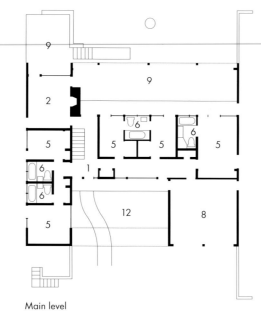

Main level

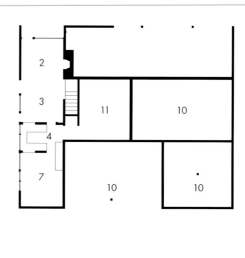

Lower level

new relationships between solid and void, with natural light transmitted to the spaces below. Filtered light, directed views, and access to the landscape remain integral to the experience of the house.

The family restored and rebuilt the house over a period of six years. In 2004 the property was sold a young couple with small children. The new owners' experience of this house is a continuation of the comfort and ease of living that the architecture provides. "Friends who visit see themselves living in a house like this," the wife observed. "They see its beauty and reflect on the light and brightness and find it inspiring. It is a space that feels elegant and natural." Soon after the purchase, the owners began to work with architect Amanda Martocchio to restore and update the guesthouse/pool house and the pool area, and they have undertaken an extensive landscaping project, which incorporated the entire property.

Current floor plan

1 Foyer
2 Living room
3 Dining room
4 Kitchen
5 Bedroom
6 Bathroom
7 Family room
8 Garage
9 Terrace
10 Unexcavated
11 Mechanical
12 Courtyard

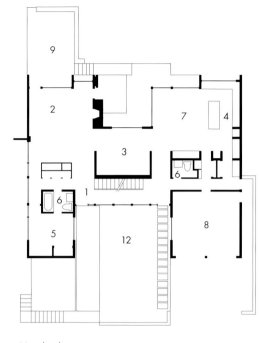

Main level

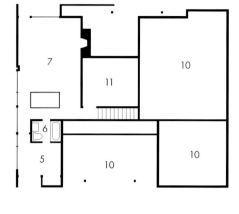

Lower level

Site plan

1 Main house
2 Terrace
3 Courtyard
4 Driveway
5 Pool house
6 Pool
7 Guesthouse

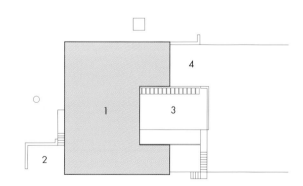

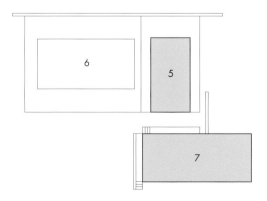

1956
Boissonnas House
Philip Johnson architect

1960
Owner 2

1971
Owner 3
Addition, pool
Philip Johnson architect

1983
Owner 4
Renovation and addition

1994
Owner 5
Restoration and preservation
Philip Johnson architect

Boissonnas House 1956 Philip Johnson

This is my best house—after my own Glass House, of course.

—Philip Johnson

Between 1949 and 1956 Philip Johnson designed six modern houses in New Canaan, beginning with the Glass House and culminating with the Boissonnas house. His colleague Richard Foster observed, "In retrospect, I can say that the houses represent a period of architectural transition and refinement for Philip. I personally view them as a series of steps in the development of the Johnson style."

The client was Eric H. Boissonnas, a geophysicist and an executive at a French engineering firm based in Ridgefield, Connecticut. Conceived as a modern interpretation of the traditional country villa, the house is much larger than other modern houses of the period and more refined in its use of materials and finishes.

The house sits on a raised terrace with views out to the surrounding woods. The plan is based on a grid of 16-foot squares, eight bays wide and five deep, with most enclosed as rooms and others left open as outdoor space. Three pavilions, a grand central space flanked by a bedroom wing on one side and a service wing on the other, make up the living space. Each is one story in height, except for the grand room, which was designed as a double-height cube. Johnson took advantage of the exposed sides of the rooms and enhanced the exterior walls with a glass wall, which not only opened the spaces to the outside but also help to frame the views, and created circulation though the house. Spaces are enclosed with large spans of glass and brick walls on which to display art.

The grid creates a compositional connection between the interior and the exterior of the house, with a series of bays defining open spaces with pergolas and patios. The use of the same materials inside and out brings the landscape into the interior, while the glass walls lend a sense of transparency and connection to nature from every room. Terraces are paved with the same brick as the interior floors, further blurring the distinction between open and enclosed spaces.

Of the thirty-eight bays, eighteen are interior spaces. One exterior bay was subsequently enclosed to enlarge the kitchen. On the exterior are twenty bays, including three terraces and five garden bays. In the exterior area of the house, the center columns of the grid disappear, as does the interior column in the great room of the house.

Eric Boissonnas sold the house in 1960, and the family relocated to France, where Johnson designed another house for them. Deeply committed to modernist architecture, Boissonnas also commissioned Marcel Breuer to design a ski resort in Switzerland, which ultimately failed.

The New Canaan house changed hands several times, and it was owned by interior designer Jay Spectre for a number of years. After his death in 1983, the house sat unwanted for two years. The current owners, who were seeking a Johnson house, were undeterred by the condition and purchased it in 1994.

Elaborate window treatment installed by a previous owner disguised the fact that all the glazing, doors, and framing needed to be replaced. Faced with the

Original floor plan

1 Foyer
2 Living room
3 Dining room
4 Kitchen
5 Bedroom
6 Bathroom
7 Garden
8 Courtyard

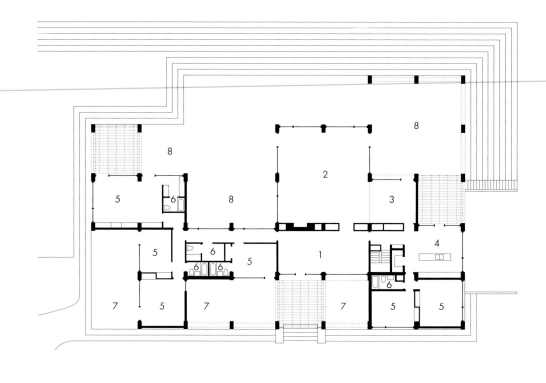

ominous realization of the need to do more work than initially envisioned, they called Philip Johnson. He graciously accepted the invitation to see the house. As the owner recalled, "Philip Johnson was charming—he came right over a few days later." Johnson revealed that when Boissonnas commissioned him to design the house, he said, "We love your Glass House, and we want a glass villa." Johnson laughed and said later, "I didn't know how to do that."

Johnson went on to explain the development of the grid: "The entry is one, the foyer is two, and the great room is four square. Once I realized that I could do that then I got it. I knew it would work. What I was really doing was breaking the Meisian cube; the grid just extends out beyond the house proper."

Following his visit, Johnson invited the owners back to the Glass House where they spent the rest of the day touring his property and seeing his art collection. The owner described spending this time with Johnson as "a magical day and an unbelievable experience. How many people get to spend three or four hours touring the Glass House property with Philip Johnson himself on a perfect summer day? I thought to myself that this was worth the price of the house."

The restoration began with the removal of the heavy drapes, excess decorations, and period details that had been added during the 1970s and 1980s. The replacement of the original glass and framing with insulated tempered glass followed. Repair of the plaster walls, refinishing of the floors, and painting came next. The flat roof and the flashing were replaced, and the pergolas restored.

The Boissonnases had furnished the house with French furniture, light sheer draperies, and traditional area rugs throughout. The new owners took their cues from the postwar period, and they have furnished it with Barcelona chairs, Le Corbusier seating, and Knoll pieces in a modern style, with works from their extensive art collection on the walls. Sculpture has been selected and installed with an eye to viewing the pieces in the round.

Current floor plan

1 Foyer
2 Living room
3 Dining room
4 Kitchen
5 Bedroom
6 Bathroom
7 Garden
8 Courtyard
9 Breakfast room
10 Study

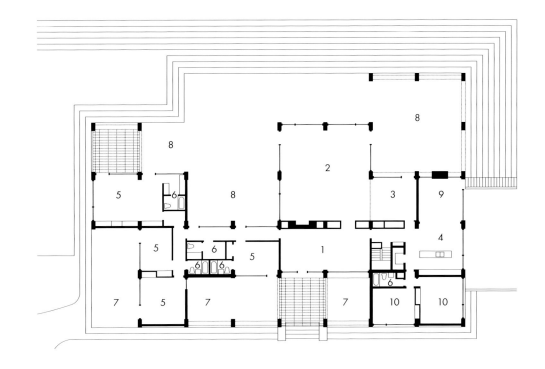

Site plan

1 Main house
2 Pool
3 Driveway
4 Terrace
5 Garden

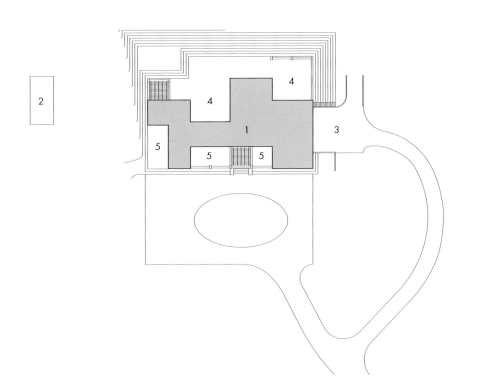

1956
Mills House 2
Willis Mills architect

1998
Owner 2
Restoration
Craig J. Bassam architect/owner

2000
Renovations
Craig J. Bassam architect/owner

2007
Owner 3
Roof restoration

Mills House 2 1956 Willis Mills

Willis Mills designed his second family residence on a dramatic steep wooded incline with ledge outcroppings. The site drops forty-five feet from the street-level entrance, and the house follows the topography, with cantilevered sections at each level. The main facade faces east and embraces the light with a two-story wall of glass spanning its length. Projecting from the facade are decks, patios, and balconies that invite inside-outside living.

What makes this house truly exceptional is the way in which the two floors relate to each other. Upon entering the foyer, the house feels open and airy as the double-height living space is revealed. A balcony allows a peek down, and the stair descends behind a massive chimney that obscures the view. At the bottom the space opens up again to reveal the full impact of the cube.

The Mills family lived in this house for more than twenty-three years, but subsequent changes in ownership took a toll on the structure. A couple, one an architect and the other a fashion ex-

ecutive, purchased the house in 1998. Following a detailed analysis of the restoration, repairs, and upgrades required, they embarked on a five-year project to bring the house back to its original state and reconfigure the space. The main level was opened up so that the space flows seamlessly from the living room to the dining room and through to the kitchen. The patio outside the living room, which reaches to the kitchen entry, gives the feeling of being in a courtyard surrounded by stone ledge. The kitchen, fitted out with natural walnut cabinets, now extends through the house, opening up to the courtyard on one side and to a deck on the other. Gleaming white terrazzo flooring replaced the original wood throughout the living spaces.

The entrance level accommodates the master suite and three additional bedrooms. During the renovation, the original garage was incorporated into the house on this level and now serves as the master suite. A freestanding gararge was built adjacent to the house. Many details were introduced to streamline the

house, including pocket doors that eliminated door swings in tight spaces. Custom millwork was restored, and the walnut paneling of the stair was extended to the kitchen, study, and master bedroom. Precise craftsmanship was important to the owners, who personally supervised the construction.

The house was sold again in 2007. For the new owner, the thoughtful and exquisitely detailed interior renovation, the views from the house out to nature, and the dramatic ledge surroundings were compelling, and he is committed to maintaining the spirit of the property.

Original floor plan

1 Foyer
2 Living room
3 Dining room
4 Kitchen
5 Bedroom
6 Bathroom
7 Study
8 Patio/Courtyard
9 Unfinished area
10 Terrace
11 Garage

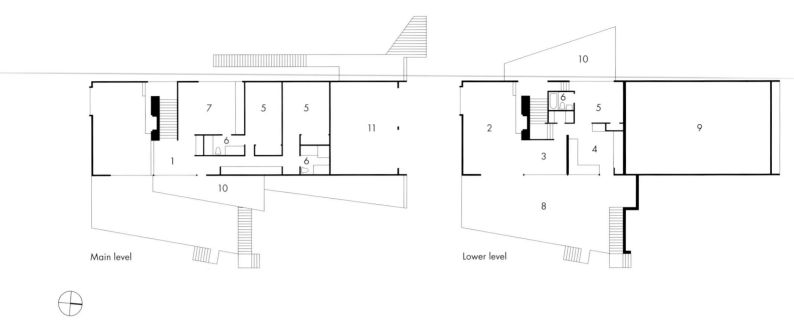

Main level

Lower level

Current floor plan

1 Foyer
2 Living room
3 Dining room
4 Kitchen
5 Bedroom
6 Bathroom
7 Study
8 Patio/Courtyard
9 Unfinished area
10 Terrace

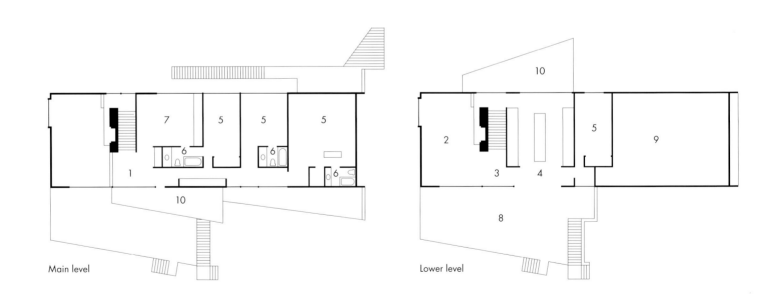

Main level

Lower level

Site plan

1 Main house
2 Garage
3 Driveway
4 Pool

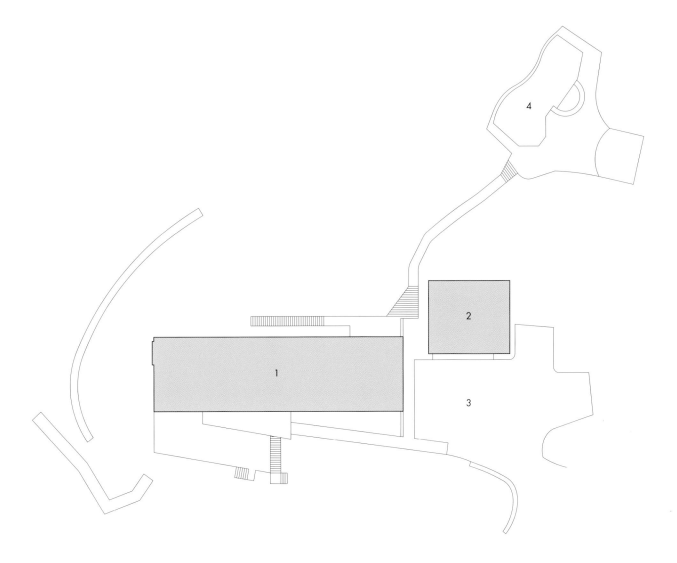

1956	1962	1969	1970	1993		2009–14
Villa Ponte	Courtyard enclosed	Swimming pool	Garage	Guesthouse	**2009**	Renovation and restoration
John Johansen architect	John Johansen architect	John Johansen architect	John Johansen architect	Morris & Morris architect	Owner 2	kitchen, site work, landscaping
						Theo Singuenza architect

Villa Ponte 1956 John Johansen

*But what has always most
interested and intrigued man
is the unusual, the exceptional,
the improvement, and change.*

—*John Johansen*

Villa Ponte was designed for Rawleigh Warner Jr., an oil executive, and his wife, Mary Ann. On John Johansen's first visit to the property, he envisioned siting the house over the stream and recommended that the Warners purchase additional land on the other side of it. The combined lots encompassed just over five wooded acres with a spur of the Rippowam River running through.

Johansen's design emerges from the classical architecture of Andrea Palladio's country villas. The plan is based on the order and organization of Palladian composition with a strong central axis and symmetrical wings. At the same time, the form of the house and its placement across the river are very much a part of the modern idiom of "form follows function" and the relationship between site and structure. In a period when the International Style vocabulary dominated modern design, Johansen experimented with the siting of the house, the relationship between its placement and its architectural expression, and the selection of materials to create a balance between modern and classical. Vaulted gold-leaf ceilings, terrazzo floors, and ebonized-wood cabinets helped to show that modernism, despite its roots in industrial efficiency, could also be luxurious.

As Johansen observed, "Of my designs, the Villa Ponte most elegantly interpreted the Palladian ideal: the central pavilion was the bridge that spanned the stream, its three bays covered by arched vaults. Flanking this bridge were secondary pavilions rendered in pink stucco decoratively embossed with my designs. Gold leaf was used in the arches and on the living room ceiling, and on the exterior spurting off rainwater to the stream below were eight gilded gargoyles designed by the sculptor Robert Engman."

The processional sequence of arrival is an essential element of the design. Sounds of rushing water greet visitors as the path descends to the entry courtyard. Inside, a small foyer and narrow passage between the wings opens into the magnificent space of the great room with its parallel walls of floor-to-ceiling glass and the stream flowing below. The sound of water and the reflections of light bounced up toward the gold-leafed vaulted ceiling are unique to this house. Polished terrazzo floors seem to contrast with the natural landscape but enrich the quality of the space.

Throughout the 1960s, the Warners worked with Johansen on projects to enclose the terrace outside the guest room, to design a naturalistic outdoor pool beside the stream, and finally to add a separate garage and pool house. The house remained in the Warner family until 1999, but it subsequently fell into disrepair.

In 2009 a young professional couple looking for a country place purchased the property. Soon after they invited Johansen to see the house once again. "You think you bought this house, but this house has bought you," Johansen observed. He fully supported their idea of a renovation and restoration, explaining that the house must evolve over time in response to its owners. "Who will tell the story at the end?

132

Original floor plan

1 Foyer
2 Living room
3 Dining room
4 Kitchen
5 Bedroom
6 Bathroom
7 Study
8 Open courtyard
9 Breakfast room
10 Terrace

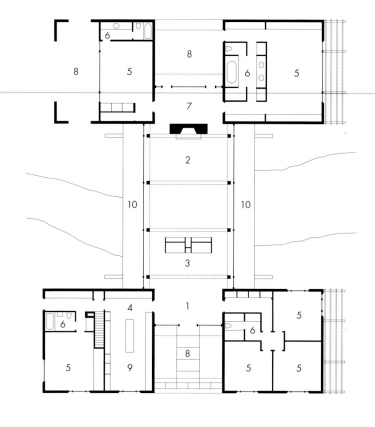

The house!" he exclaimed. The owners found inspiration in his words and began their journey.

Working with architect Theo Singuenza, the new owners approached the project in phases, with a commitment to preserving the integrity of Johansen's design. The interiors have been transformed while keeping their use as originally intended. New custom cabinetry and the restoration of the original wood have enhanced the sense of luxury, as have the new glass walls trimmed in mahogany, a new copper vaulted roof, and the plate-glass balcony fronts that project over the river.

A new winding, tree-lined driveway has transformed the approach to the house. Trees and shrubs have been carefully selected to enhance the senses—a weeping hemlock tree from the 1950s and an ornamental katsura tree opposite the main entrance. "Landscaping is deceptively simple," the owner explained, "but it actually takes more effort to create plantings that will bring the landscape back to the architect's initial design intentions." Here the land and river are integrated with the house in a unique way. The luxuriant canopy of trees, the elegant wooden bridges, and the meandering paths create a truly majestic setting.

Current floor plan

1 Foyer
2 Living room
3 Dining room
4 Kitchen
5 Bedroom
6 Bathroom
7 Study
8 Open courtyard
9 Breakfast room
10 Terrace
11 Office

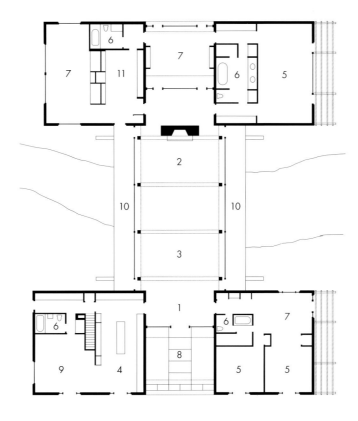

Site plan

1 Main house
2 Pool
3 Guesthouse
4 River
5 Driveway

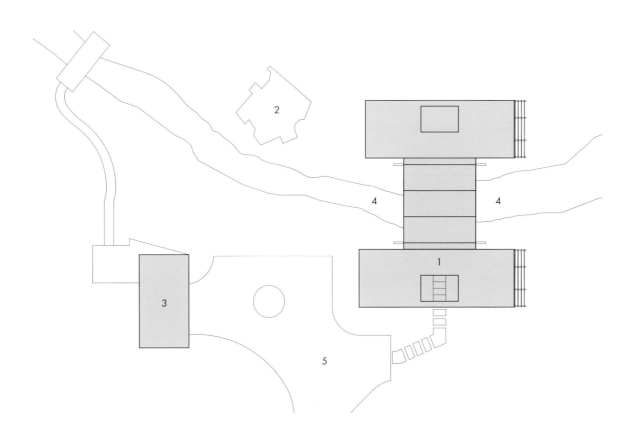

1957
Celanese House
Edward Durell Stone architect

1960
Owner 1

2006
Owner 2
Restoration and addition

2008
Owner 3
Renovation and restoration
Nicholas Karytinos architect

2008
Site work and landscape
Stephen Lederach
landscape architet

Celanese House 1957 Edward Durell Stone

I try to find architecture that is hopefully timeless, free of the mannerisms of the moment. Architecture should follow a grander and more ageless pattern and it can and should be approached simply.

—Edward Durell Stone

The story of the Celanese house began in 1957, with a joint venture between the Celanese Corporation of America and Theodore Hobbs, a New Canaan builder, to create a show house to display state-of-the-art products manufactured by Celanese. Hobbs acquired the site, and Celanese selected the architect and the interior designers. Under the terms of the contract, Hobbs committed to construct a modern house, which was to be sold following the advertising campaign. The project was named "The American Idea," which was intended to embody the spirit in the nation during the 1950s pursuit of the American Dream.

Edward Durell Stone was awarded the commission to design the house. By the late 1950s, his style had evolved from a stark modernism to a more decorative, ornamental approach that gave this house a softer character in comparison to many other modern houses in New Canaan.

The house is nested on the property, down from the road. The single-story structure is wrapped in a geometrical lace screen that encloses both the structure and the private courtyards. Pyramidal skylights stand in rigid rows on the roof, adding to the intrigue. The plan is based a modular grid, with an axial relationship from front to back of open living areas and two transverse axes, one connecting the living areas and the other the private areas. The main house was organized into three zones: the dining room, kitchen, and master bedroom to the north; entry and living area in the center; and two bedrooms and a study on the south. A covered dining courtyard was originally inserted in the space between the kitchen and the garage. The original finishes reflected the Celanese Corporation's line of products, which included many different types of building materials, including wall board, trim, linoleum, carpets, adhesives, paints, fabrics, and furnishings.

In 1960 Frederick and Velma Willcox purchased the house, and Mrs. Willcox lived there until her death in 2005. An intermediate owner sold the property to the present owners, who have restored the building and integrated the landscape, working with architect Nicholas Karytinos and landscape architect Stephen Lederach.

A rectilinear planting of linden trees flanking the entry now extends the geometry of the house into the forecourt. Trimmed to align with the roof, the trees connect directly to the architecture, creating a leafy canopy. As Lederach explained, "Our vision was to create a space that embraced the architecture, took its cues from it, and extended that relationship to the exterior, accomplishing this within the parameters that you could achieve sustainable design within a formal presentation." At the back of the house, the landscape surrounding the terrace is now framed by a meadow to the east and a colonnade of trees to the north.

Within the house itself, the owners sought to create a balance between the old and the new. The linoleum has been replaced with a satin bleached oak, natural-finish wood floor throughout. The floor brings warmth to the space, and the contrast between the floors and the

Original floor plan

1 Foyer
2 Living room
3 Dining room
4 Kitchen
5 Bedroom
6 Bathroom
7 Study
8 Terrace
9 Garage
10 Courtyard
11 Reflection pool
12 Family room

stark white walls and ceilings heightens the sense of sophistication and calm. Sliding glass walls have been replaced in keeping with the proportions and thermal properties of building materials available today. Floor-to-ceiling bookshelves in the original dining area and study now house an impressive art reference library.

The kitchen has been redesigned to flow with the needs of the family, and the cabinets were selected to blend in with the tone and decor of the house. A custom flat skylight now balances the light with the adjacent rooms. As the owner observed, "There is a subtle light that enters the rooms through these skylights. The design integrates a floating panel that conceals the skylight from the interior and also serves to diffuse and distribute light throughout the room. Light can change the color of the walls depending on how it reflects on the surface."

Karytinos concurred: "The natural light in the space captures you and surprises you. The ceilings are only eight feet high, but you feel the airiness and lightness of a much grander space. The light in itself evokes an emotion; the way it bounces off the walls and ceilings emphasizes their purpose, which is to deliver light in the most efficient way possible."

Today the house is flawless in its execution, with a sensibility that aims to improve and not detract, maintaining the balance and integrity of the original design while allowing the house to evolve into a space designed for tomorrow.

Current floor plan

1 Foyer
2 Living room
3 Dining room
4 Kitchen
5 Bedroom
6 Bathroom
7 Study
8 Terrace
9 Garage
10 Courtyard
11 Laundry room

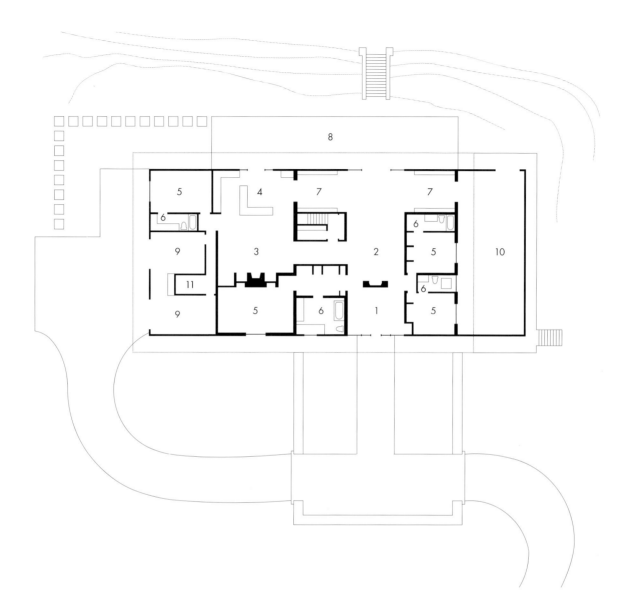

1957
Irwin Pool House
Landis Gores architect

2005
Owner 2
Preservation
New Canaan Historical Society

2006
Restoration
William D. Earls architect

Irwin Pool House (now Gores Pavilion) 1957 Landis Gores

Jane Watson Irwin and her husband, John N. Irwin, a lawyer and diplomat who served in the Eisenhower, Nixon, and Johnson administrations, commissioned Landis Gores to design a pool house for their estate in New Canaan. The property, which encompassed approximately thirty-six acres with rolling lawns, apple orchards, many specimen plantings, and a Tudor-style house, along with stables, barns, and other outbuildings, was a gift to the couple from Mrs. Irwin's parents, Jeanette K. Watson and Thomas J. Watson Sr., founder of IBM.

Jack Irwin met Landis Gores in the Army Reserve, and the two became good friends. Coincidentally the wives of both men were from New Canaan families, and the two couples settled in town.

The pool house reflects Gores's interest in the International Style and in the architecture of Frank Lloyd Wright. The form of the building, a cross-axial composition built on a shallow plinth, and the glazed walls are clearly modernist elements, while the hipped slate roof with

deep overhangs and particularly the massive Prairie-style fireplace are derived from Wright.

The focal point of the pool house is the main central room, which boasts movable high glass walls, high ceilings, and an unobstructed view of the surrounding landscape. The fireplace, constructed in a dove-gray brick, manually cleft by the Appalachian Shale Company and finished with wide bluestone mantels, is a simple presentation of juxtaposed planes in different depths. Located toward the back of the room, with a deep and high hearth, the fireplace seems to float as it divides the main space from the kitchen behind. Materials include terrazzo-like Armstrong tiles and custom spacing strips on the floor and custom-milled redwood horizontal boarding on the walls. The terraces are paved in bluestone.

Symmetrical wings extend on either side of the central pavilion; originally each wing included its own bathroom, shower, and changing rooms. These were converted to bedrooms when the

Irwins began to use the building as a weekend retreat.

In 2005 the Town of New Canaan purchased the property for passive recreation and parkland. The pool was filled in, but, thanks to the efforts of the New Canaan Historical Society, the pool house was preserved and restored. William D. Earls was selected as the architect for this project, which took two years to complete. The new program for the building included a multimedia exhibition room, an exhibit gallery, storage, pantry, a grand room for lectures and social events, and public restrooms. During the construction, the structural system of the roof over the wings was exposed, adding significant height to the spaces. Indirect lighting accentuates the truss system. Period materials and finishes were sourced, including the Armstrong terrazzo vinyl tile and spacers on the floors.

The great room is furnished in period furniture original to the house, complemented by a pair of sofas designed specially for the space by the well-known furniture design pioneer Jens Risom.

Original floor plan

1 Foyer
2 Great room
3 Changing room
4 Kitchen
5 Bathroom
6 Boiler room
7 Pool

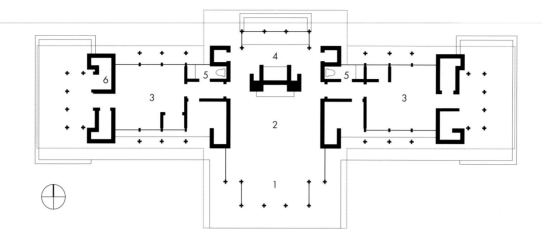

In 2011 the building was dedicated as the Landis Gores Pavilion, and it is now operated by the New Canaan Historical Society as a gallery displaying works of and films on the Harvard Five and other architects, designers, and photographers of the period.

Current floor plan

1 Foyer
2 Great room
3 Exhibit room
4 Kitchen
5 Bathroom
6 Boiler room

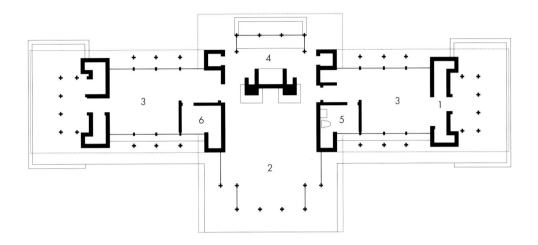

Site plan

1 Gores Pavilion
2 Driveway/Parking
3 Main entrance
4 Walking paths

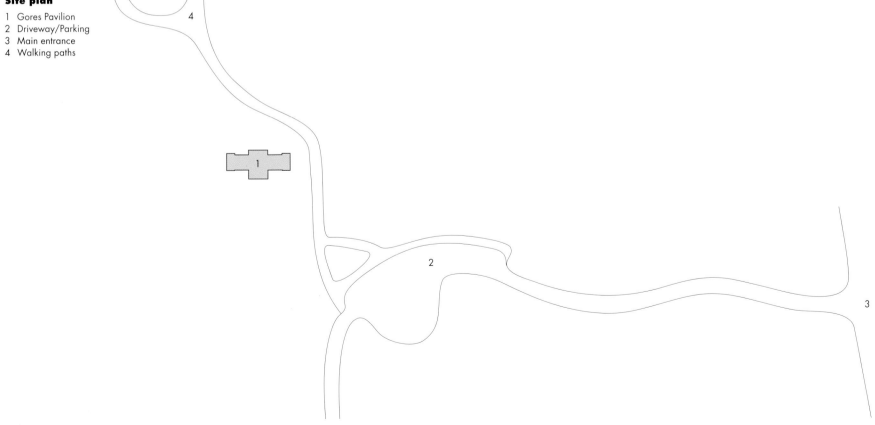

1962
Tatum House
Hugh Smallen architect

1967
Addition south wing
Hugh Smallen architect

1970
Addition barn garage
Hugh Smallen architect

1995
Owner 2
Removal of outdoor sculpture

1999
Owner 3

2010
Addition kitchen, bathroom
John Black Lee architect

2012
Storage shed, carport
Alan Goldberg architect

Tatum House 1962 Hugh Smallen

Hugh Smallen designed this house for Liston and Corinne Tatum and their three sons with the goal of creating maximum living space for a modest budget. The house stands in a clearing surrounded by woods on a two-acre lot with a stream running through it. Originally a simple rectangle in plan, it is a one-story structure with a flat roof. The design and detailing are typical of Smallen's work. The space was designed to maximize efficiency and natural light. Like many midcentury architects, Smallen was committed to limiting walls within the interior to create larger spaces that could function as multipurpose rooms. Freestanding cabinetry was used to articulate different uses within the same room. In the Tatum house, a large custom wardrobe originally separated the dining from the living room. The cabinetry did not reach the ceiling, defining the spaces without enclosing them or blocking the light. Along the perimeter, floor-to-ceiling window walls not only provided a view, but, more importantly, they also created the illusion of larger rooms.

In 1967 the Tatums commissioned Smallen to extend the house, adding a wing on the south side that transformed the plan into a T. Since the addition disrupted the symmetry of the front facade, Smallen also added low exterior freestanding walls to the north end to restore balance, but these were subsequently removed after the Tatums sold the house in the mid-1990s.

In 1999 Craig Bloom and Ashlea Ebeling, a young couple living in a modern loft space in New York City, ventured to New Canaan to scout real estate for future consideration. Winter had set in and it was lightly snowing as they came up to the Tatum house. "I loved the winter feeling in the space," Bloom recalled. "We weren't planning on buying at all, but we found ourselves, two days after seeing this house, making an offer."

To guide their decisions in developing a restoration strategy, the couple acquired a set of photographs by Ezra Stoller taken in 1963, shortly after the house was completed. Ultimately they opted to divide the project into three phases, the first phase starting in 2003 and the entire project lasting until 2009. For the first phase, they retained John Black Lee, an accomplished midcentury modern architect. His assignment was to work within the footprint of the wing to create a living room from a study and renovate the master suite.

In 2010 they started on phase two, which focused on the kitchen. The owners did much of the material selection and, with the assistance of their general contractor, took on the project of interior design and restoration. "We worked with Bulthaup to design the kitchen and followed with selecting materials for the bathrooms," Bloom explained. "In retrospect it was largely our vision and collaboration with Alan Peterman, our builder/general contractor on execution. We knew what we liked, but did not yet have the sense of how things came together."

Changes to the plan proposed by Lee have enhanced the flow of space that characterized the original house. A wall that once enclosed the kitchen has been

Original floor plan

1 Foyer
2 Living room
3 Dining room
4 Kitchen
5 Bedroom
6 Bathroom
7 Office
8 Terrace
9 Storage

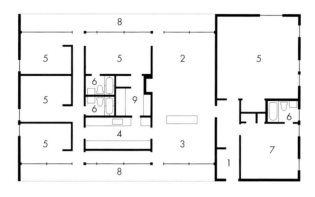

removed and a hallway reclaimed to expand the visual connection between the kitchen and the outdoors. The bedrooms have remained the same, but the closets have been customized to maximize storage and minimize the need for furniture. The bathrooms have been completely transformed into a more modern aesthetic.

The original materials used to anchor the house are seen in the wooden ceiling and the wood floors, and they remain as fresh today as when the house was built. The floor-to-ceiling glass walls open the house and brighten the rooms with light that reflects off the white walls and spills onto all the surfaces, while enlarged skylights also introduce natural light. Walkways that project out from the house help to blur the line between indoors and out.

To improve the grounds, the couple approached Peter Rolland, a landscape architect who had often collaborated with Smallen. At his suggestion, a stand of white birch trees was planted along the entry path, relating to the color and geometry of the house and at the same time connecting it to the landscape. Rolland also installed a border of smooth black river rocks at the base of the building to maintain the crisp line of the white perimeter.

The most recent undertaking was to resolve the driveway and approach to the house. Alan Goldberg designed a structural but sculptural carport with some of the parking areas covered and others open, as well as a freestanding sophisticated storage area. Both the architect and the landscape architect worked to bring their respective visions together and

complement the house. The landscape and the sculptural element add a new level of sophistication to the property that enhances the composition and presentation of the house.

Current floor plan

1 Foyer
2 Living room
3 Dining room
4 Kitchen
5 Bedroom
6 Bathroom
7 Study
8 Terrace
9 Storage
10 Family room
11 Carport

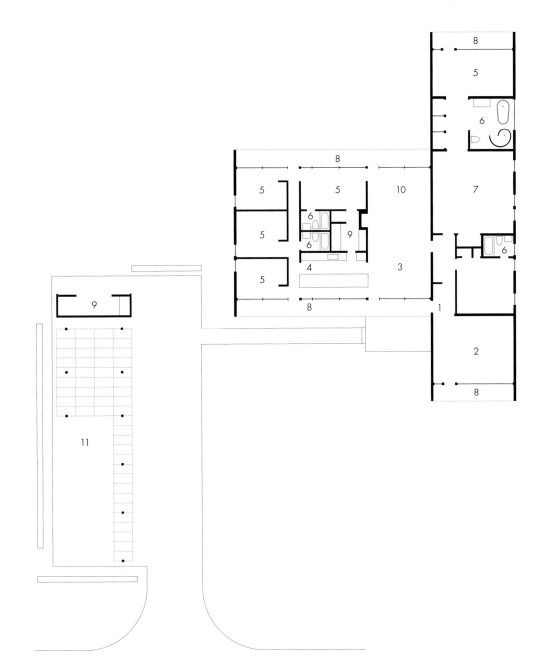

1962
Birkenstock House
Victor Christ-Janer architect

1970
Fire reconstruction

1990
Owner 2

1994
Owner 3

2003
Addition and renovation
J. P. Franzen architect

Birkenstock House 1962 Victor Christ-Janer

I am interested in the feelings as they are evoked from the experiential nature of architecture.

—Victor Christ-Janer

Victor Christ-Janer designed this house for James W. Birkenstock, an IBM executive, and his wife, Jean, who moved to New Canaan to raise their young family in 1952. The four-and-one-quarter acre site included the man-made Blueberry Pond, which became the pivotal reference point for the setting of the house.

Under the aegis of Eliot Noyes, IBM developed a corporate branding strategy and product image focusing on art, architectural design, and artistic value. This approach influenced the many executives who lived in New Canaan to emulate the "modern life" that the company was building on, and the Birkenstocks' choice of a modernist architect was part of the trend.

Originally the house was a single story with a low-pitched roof and deep overhangs. A window wall, which spanned the entire rear facade, opened onto a large curving concrete terrace overlooking the pond. A fire destroyed a portion of the house facing the pond in 1970, and the house was rebuilt within that year. In 1990 the Birkenstocks bequeathed the

house to Fairfield University, which sold it to the present owners four years later.

In 2002 the present owners commissioned J. P. Franzen Associates Architects to renovate and expand the house. Franzen had worked for many years in Christ-Janer's office before setting up his own practice, which gave him firsthand knowledge of Christ-Janer's design approach as well as experience in working with the local zoning regulations. At that time, zoning regulations limited the expansion of the building footprint and restricted any use or construction of independent outbuildings.

The goal of the project was to preserve the spirit of the house, while expanding the private living space and updating and improving its infrastructure. A second level was added, incorporating operable ribbon windows that replicated the scale of the existing fenestration. The addition has a flat roof, which is more in character with the International Style than the original design.

The layout and circulation through

the house are close to the original plan except for the space now occupied by the stair connecting the main and upper levels. With the family bedrooms now located upstairs, the original bedrooms on the main level have been adapted to other uses, including a library, an exercise room, and a storage room. The main entrance, once recessed in the facade, has been moved forward, and a new portico projects out from the house to shelter and accentuate it.

The interiors are filled with natural light and offer long, unobstructed views of the pond and landscape. Clear-finished white-oak floors are covered with area rugs in solid colors that complement the classical modern furnishings, including designs by Mies van der Rohe and Knoll. The rooms display a collection of contemporary and Asian art that enriches the space with color and movement.

Although the house has been altered, the feeling of living in the modern aesthetic has not changed, and living modern is still the credo for this family.

Original floor plan

1 Foyer
2 Living room
3 Dining room
4 Kitchen
5 Bedroom
6 Bathroom
7 Mud room
8 Patio
9 Storage
10 Family room
11 Garage
12 Center hall

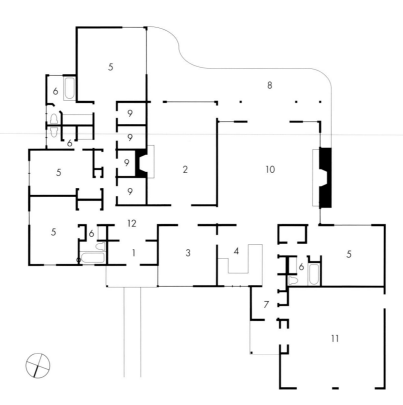

Current floor plan

1 Foyer
2 Living room
3 Dining room
4 Kitchen
5 Bedroom
6 Bathroom
7 Mud room
8 Patio
9 Storage
10 Family room
11 Garage
12 Central hall
13 Library
14 Exercise room

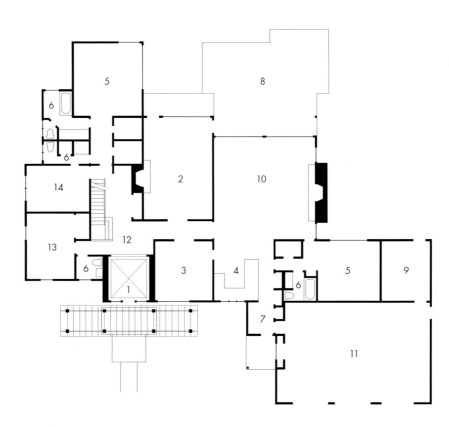

Site plan

1 Main house
2 Driveway
3 Shed
4 Patio
5 Lake
6 Pool

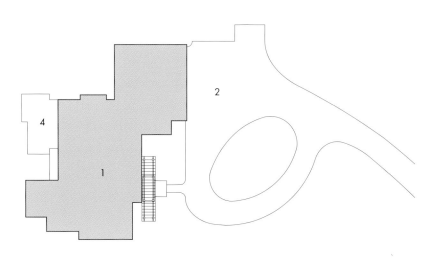

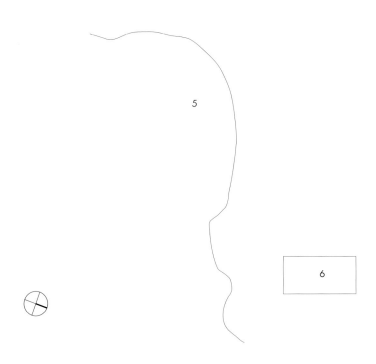

1963
Becker House
Hugh Smallen

2003
Owner 2

2004
Renovation

2005
Kitchen renovation

2005
Owner 3

Becker House 1963 Hugh Smallen

Nathaniel and Theo Becker, founders of Becker & Becker Associates, a facilities research and architectural planning consulting firm, commissioned their friend Hugh Smallen to design a house for them and their three sons. The two-and-one-half acre property, adjacent to Smallen's own residence, encompassed a large leveled area on grade with the road and a steep hillside slope, with a meandering stream separating it from a lower flat area of land.

The house is sited at the front of the property, close to the driveway. In front, a tall 60-foot-long fieldstone wall is an imposing and protective presence. A narrow opening just off center leads to the house itself. To the left, a second fieldstone wall, perpendicular to the front wall, directs visitors to the front door and conceals the carport. To the right is a garden courtyard beneath a pergola. The house is clad in wide vertical siding with floor-to-ceiling windows on both the front and rear facades.

Smallen nestled the house into the hill,

creating a full two-story house on a stone base at the rear. Living spaces are on the first level with private areas below. The focal point of the interior is a two-story wall behind an open sculptural stair leading to the lower level. The house is compact, efficient, open, and bright, with maximum privacy on all sides.

In developing the plan, Smallen originally created a structural grid, which he used to establish the building envelope, and then he broke it down to overcome its limitations. On the main level, the plan for the public areas is open, interrupted only by the stairwell and a wall separating the service spaces—kitchen, bathroom, and study—from it. Even the placement of these two elements does not follow the grid, allowing fluid circulation. A freestanding custom cabinetry wall, designed by Jens Risom, acts as a divider between the living and dining spaces without interrupting the flow of space or light.

In contrast, on the lower level, full-height walls define the bedrooms according to the grid, with the fourth wall

in glass. The open view toward the back of the property makes all the bedrooms feel private, open, and much larger than their actual size.

On the main level, windows and balconies that punctuate the back and side walls frame the views out onto the landscape. On the sides of the house, narrow vertical windows and balconies with sliding doors admit natural light without compromising privacy. On the front, the glass wall in the living room faces the street, but interior privacy is ensured by the stone wall, which seems almost impenetrable. There is both a sense of freedom of space and a feeling of protectiveness applied subtly and effectively that offers a modern lifestyle without sacrificing privacy or comfort.

The Beckers sold the house in 2002, and subsequent owners updated and modified the original floor plan at both levels without increasing its overall footprint. To enlarge the bedrooms, two were eliminated and their area was incorporated into the rooms that remain.

Original floor plan

1 Foyer
2 Living room
3 Dining room
4 Kitchen
5 Bedroom
6 Bathroom
7 Play room
8 Carport
9 Courtyard
10 Covered walkway
11 Balcony
12 Storage

Main level   Lower level

The kitchen and bedroom on the main level were partially combined to allow for a more open area. Windows were updated and a balcony installed off the dining room area.

The current owners, who purchased the property in 2005, are working toward returning the house to its original configuration. The interiors are accented by the use of color. A deep-blue two-story wall is a foil to the sculptural stair between the two levels. A deep orange draws attention toward the living room area. The bold application of color gives a vibrant feeling of life that infuses and energizes the space. The house is furnished with a growing collection of midcentury pieces that include the designs of Breuer, Eames, Risom, and others.

"A house like this one is a way of living," the owner observed. "Perhaps it's the views and the visual connection to the outside that builds connection within the family."

"We love that the house is small by today's standards and that it feels like it treads lightly on its surroundings," he added. "A modern house is like a blank canvas: you need to be inventive in using the space—the house requires you to let go and be yourself."

Current floor plan

1 Foyer
2 Living room
3 Dining room
4 Kitchen
5 Bedroom
6 Bathroom
7 Study
8 Carport
9 Courtyard
10 Covered walkway
11 Balcony
12 Storage

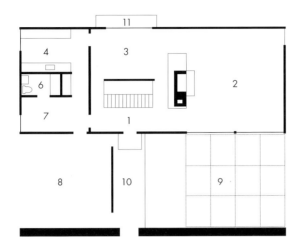

Main level

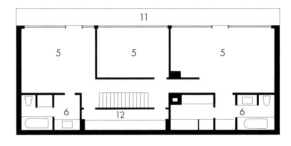

Lower level

1952
John Johansen architect

1966
Owner 2

1977
Goldberg House
Addition
Alan Goldberg architect

1979
Carport
Alan Goldberg architect

2007
Addition
Alan Goldberg architect

Goldberg House 1977 Alan Goldberg

Modern architecture can take so many forms and shapes, but it should be looking to the future not the past.

—Alan Goldberg

After more than ten years of working in New York architecture offices, Alan Goldberg moved to New Canaan to join Eliot Noyes in 1966. He and his wife purchased a house designed in 1952 for Paschall and Betsy Campbell by John Johansen. The house was a classic International Style structure—one story with a flat roof and a compact layout—and built on a modest budget with a materials-conscious approach. Its sloping site was beautifully landscaped by Paschall Campbell, who was a well-known landscape architect.

The Goldbergs recognized that the house was very efficiently designed but small, and they intended to add to it eventually. When the original materials began to reach the end of their lifespan in the late 1970s, the Goldbergs embarked on plans for a renovation and expansion.

Goldberg kept the symmetry of the house and the spirit of its design, with the typical separation of public and private spaces. A new wing with a basement was added to the living room, extending its width and almost doubling the square footage of the house. The private space was also expanded by four feet in width as the bedrooms were too small by today's standard. An exterior courtyard on the back of the house was enclosed to increase the living areas without extending the footprint.

On the exterior, the house was resided with vertical redwood boards that were painted white, and all doors and windows were replaced with the latest energy efficiencies. Expansive glass walls frame the view out from the living room to the forested landscape that steeply descends from the house. A cantilevered terrace outside the living room seems to sit in the treetops that surround the property. In 1979 A carport was also added to the front courtyard, but it is concealed from the street by large rock outcroppings on the site.

In 2007 the house underwent another major change when a new wing was added connecting to the main house via a glass-enclosed bridge that further defines the courtyard. The addition includes a master bedroom suite, a study, storage, and a long passage to the living room. The passage is fully glazed and open to the landscape at the back of the house.

The detailing of this house is sophisticated and timeless—subtle and true to the International Style. Interior materials reflect the New England idiom: bluestone floors, fieldstone walls, and stained natural wood on the ceilings. A freestanding fireplace anchors the house but allows light and air to circulate easily. Finely detailed cabinetry throughout the house make the spaces truly warm and sophisticated.

Furnishings include pieces by Knoll, Scarpa, Eames, Mies, Nelson, and Breuer, complemented by custom pieces designed by Goldberg. An extensive collection of Mexican folk art in a wide range of media adds vibrancy and color to the space.

The Goldbergs have now lived in the house for nearly fifty years. They have loved the property, the house, and the history and legacy that they have created there.

Original floor plan

1 Foyer
2 Living room
3 Dining room
4 Kitchen
5 Bedroom
6 Bathroom
7 Terrace
8 Garden

Current floor plan

1　Foyer
2　Living room
3　Dining room
4　Kitchen
5　Bedroom
6　Bathroom
7　Terrace
8　Study
9　Closet
10　Carport
11　Parking area
12　Driveway

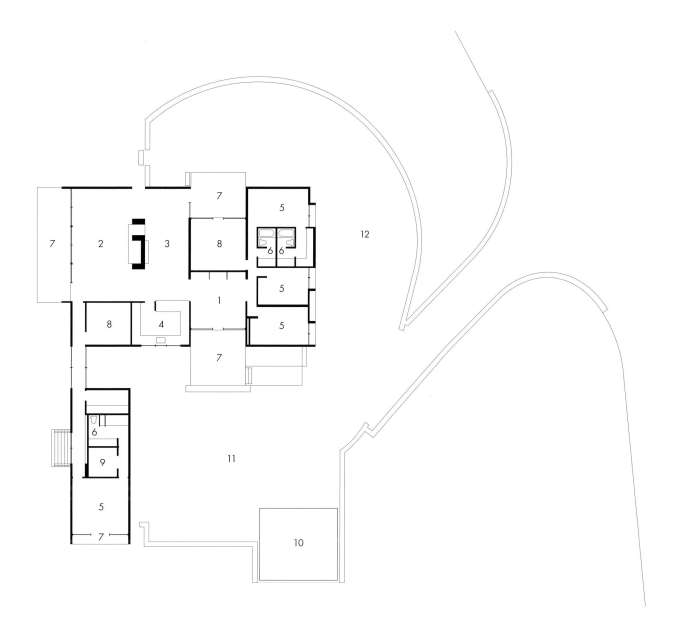

1978
Chivvis House
Eliot Noyes architect

1982
Addition and garage
Alan Goldberg architect

2008
Guesthouse
and site plan
Alan Goldberg architect

Chivvis House 1978 Eliot Noyes

Built for Lyn and Arthur Chivvis, this was the last house that Eliot Noyes designed. The commission was particularly significant because Lyn Chivvis had grown up in the house Noyes designed for her parents, Nina and Paul Bremer, in 1951. The Bremers were friends with the New Canaan architects—Paul played chess with Marcel Breuer—and their house was a gathering place for the group.

In planning their own house, the Chivvises were more interested in Noyes's house as a precedent. Noyes had played an active role in the real estate search and selected this property, which is close to his own. The aspects of the site that attracted Noyes were its secluded location at the end of a private road, with a bridge across a meandering brook at the entrance and a hill rising beyond.

Preliminary discussions about the design took place at the Noyes house. Noyes wanted to give them their own design and identity, but he kept in mind the details of his house that they admired. The Chivvises had small children, and much of

the discussion focused on accommodating the needs of a young family. "You know instinctively what will work and what won't," Lyn Chivvis observed. "We were pretty outspoken about it, and El would listen and find a solution."

As built, the Chivvis house has many elements that are hallmarks of Noyes design. The house is set deep into the site, presenting as a group of buildings carefully arranged across manicured lawns in perfect relationship with each other. Fieldstone walls and bluestone walks punctuate the landscape.

The main house is a classic combination of fieldstone walls, vertical wood siding, glass window walls sheltered by deep overhangs, and bluestone floors. In plan the house consists of two wings, one public and the other private, flanking the courtyard with a corridor connecting them across the back.

"On the day we moved in, I didn't get here until after dark," Lyn Chivvis said. "I remember driving up over the hill. Every single light was on, and it was so beautiful!"

The interior finishes also echo the Noyes house, with the same slate floors and warm oak cabinetry and bookcases. The massive fireplace is also original to Noyes, built of fieldstone with a heavy limestone hearth. Breuer gave the couple a pair of andirons he designed for them as a housewarming present. From inside, the view out from either side of the living room is of the woods with a dramatic drop in elevation. Interior window walls overlook the courtyard and the fieldstone wall that shields the private wing.

The interior of the house is furnished with traditional oriental carpets, heirloom family pieces, and midcentury designs by Breuer, Eames, Pfister, Nelson, and Le Corbusier. Artwork is displayed throughout the house alongside family heirlooms and photographs.

Noyes died before the house was completed. A few years later, when the Chivvises were interested in expanding the house and building a guesthouse and garage, they consulted Alan Goldberg, the managing partner of the Noyes

Original floor plan

1 Foyer
2 Living room
3 Dining room
4 Kitchen
5 Bedroom
6 Bathroom
7 Storage
8 Courtyard

Current floor plan

1 Foyer
2 Living room
3 Dining room
4 Kitchen
5 Bedroom
6 Bathroom
7 Storage
8 Courtyard
9 Study
10 Office
11 Terrace
12 Garage
13 Driveway

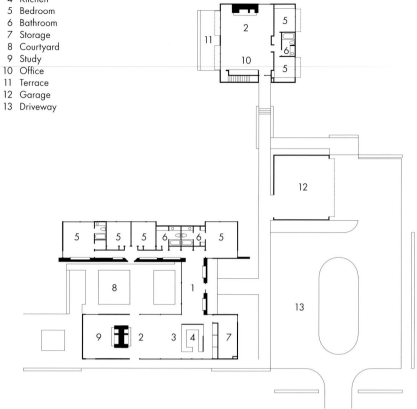

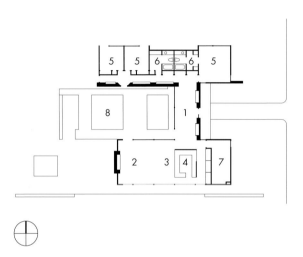

office. Goldberg extended both wings of the main house, creating a study/den on the other side of the fireplace and he added an additional bedroom to the private wing. In 2008 Goldberg designed a guesthouse and a garage. A site plan was also developed to unify all the buildings and create a coherent connection between them and the landscape. Goldberg's design builds on Noyes's ideas and unifies the various elements in a careful balance between original and new.

Site plan

1 Main house
2 Driveway
3 Garage
4 Guesthouse
5 Courtyard

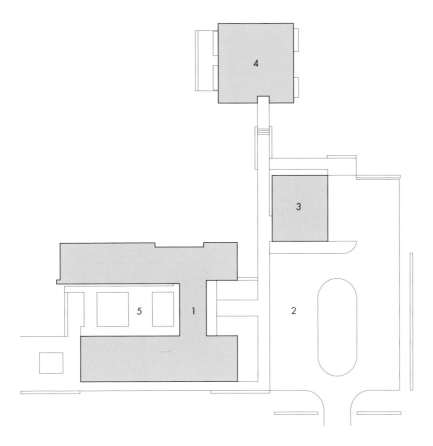

Acknowledgments

We wish to thank and acknowledge all who supported this project, as they have made this work richer in scope and insight.

We acknowledge the invaluable contributions of all those who assisted in the discovery and development process that included research, data collection, site preparation, staging, presentations, support, and drawings. For their efforts and unwavering encouragement, we salute and thank Eliza Bedell, Bruce Becker, John Black Lee, Susan Bishop, Robert Bishop, Katherine Christ-Janer, Karey Christ-Janer, Craig Bloom, Gordon Bruce, Sally Bruce, Charles Burleigh, Arthur Chivvis, Lyn Chivvis, Carrie Collangelo, Robert Damora, Circa Damora, William Earls, Ashlea Ebeling, Michael Fedele, Roger Ferris, Amy Franzen, John Franzen, Paul Galloway, Richard Geist, Dixie Gerrero, Alan Goldberg, Gertrude Goldberg, Pam Gores, Michael Hobbs, Christen Johansen, Tracy Karl, Janet Lindstrom, Raymond Matz, Donna Matz, Doug Marshall, Joeb Moore, Fred Noyes, Gay French-Ottaviani, Dave Prutting, Jens Risom, Marty Skrelunas, Kris Steele, Inger Stringfellow, Jack Triffero, Prudy Parris, Lauren Ross, Martin Ross, and Hicks Stone.

This book would not have been possible without the generosity and commitment of the owners who opened their houses to us and willingly shared their experiences, perspective, and memories. These interviews greatly enhanced our understanding of each architect's vision and design, and the additional information gathered provided broader historical context that in turn led us to other sources for further investigation. The owners were integral partners in affirming the collective preservation of these beautiful midcentury modern houses.

Equally committed to the mission of preservation through their own respective stewardship efforts, collections, and documentation are the following institutions to which we are also indebted: New Canaan Historical Society, Glass House, Museum of Modern Art, and the Town of New Canaan.

Additionally, we wish to recognize the work of the photographers of that period whose film captured images that transformed architecture into striking still art form. Within this body of visual documentation are the photographs of Robert Damora, Pedro Guerrero, Ezra Stoller, and Nina Bremer.

Above all, we thank our editor, Elizabeth White, for her expert guidance throughout this project and The Monacelli Press for the opportunity to bring this book from concept to publication.

Words cannot express our gratitude to our agents Carolyn French for believing in the project from the start, and to Peter Sawyer of Fifi Oscard Agency for running with it. This book would not have been possible if not for their support and leadership.

Lastly, we honor the architects and designers of this period whose creations inspired us. With collaboration comes motivation. The contributions of many have given voice to an important segment of architectural history and illustrated its intrinsic worth. It is therefore our sincere hope that this book will serve as a catalyst for renewed engagement in preservation efforts.

Selected Bibliography

Bruce, Gordon. *Eliot Noyes: A Pioneer of Design and Architecture in the Age of American Modernism*. London; New York: Phaidon, 2006.

Christ-Janer, Victor F. "Constituent Imagery." *Perspecta 17* (1980): 8–17.

Droste, Magdalena. *Bauhaus, 1919–1933*. Cologne: Taschen, 1993.

Earls, William E. *The Harvard Five in New Canaan: Midcentury Modern Houses by Marcel Breuer, Landis Gores, John Johansen, Philip Johnson, Eliot Noyes & Others*. New York: W. W. Norton, 2006.

Frampton, Kenneth. *Modern Architecture: A Critical History*. London; New York: Thames & Hudson, 2007.

Gatje, Robert. *Marcel Breuer: A Memoir*. New York: The Monacelli Press, 2000.

Gores, Landis, and Richard Foster. "Philip Johnson in New Canaan: The Glass House." In *New Canaan Historical Society Annual*. New Canaan: New Canaan Historical Society, 1986.

Gores, Landis, Papers. New Canaan Historical Society Library.

Greenwich Times. "Victor Frederick Christ-Janer." April 17, 2008.

Guerrero, Pedro E. *Pedro E. Guerrero: A Photographer's Journey*. New York: Princeton Architectural Press, 2007.

Hardwood, John. *The Interface: IBM and the Transformation of Corporate Design, 1945–1976*. Minneapolis: University of Minnesota Press, 2011.

Hitchcock, Henry-Russell, and Philip Johnson. *The International Style*. New York: W. W. Norton & Co., 1932.

House & Home. "Celanese House." July 1959.

"Good Design is Good Business." IBM's 100 Icons of Progress, featured March 8, 2011. http://www-03.ibm.com/ibm/history/ibm100/us/en/icons/gooddesign.

Jenkins, Stover, and David Mohney. *The Houses of Philip Johnson*. New York: Abbeville Press, 2001.

Johansen, John. "Art and Behavior in Architecture." *Perspecta 7* (1961): 43–50.

Johnson, Philip. *The Philip Johnson Tapes: Interviews by Robert A. M. Stern*. New York: The Monacelli Press, 2008.

Kristal, Marc. "Pursuing Perfection." *Dwell 5*, no. 4 (March 2005): 112–19.

Landis Gores. New Canaan: New Canaan Historical Society, n.d.

Life Magazine. "A House for All Seasons." February 15, 1963.

Lippert, Kevin. "Introduction." In John MacLane Johansen. *Nanoarchitecture: A New Species of Architecture*. New York: Princeton Architectural Press, 2002.

Modern Home Survey, New Canaan, Connecticut. National Trust for Historic Preservation.

New York Times. "Hugh Jerome Smallen Jr., Architect, 71." June 15, 1990.

New York Times. "Willis N. Mills, 88, A Civic Architect." September 24, 1995.

Property Assessors Files, Town of New Canaan.

Stone, Hicks. *Edward Durell Stone: A Son's Untold Story of a Legendary Architect*. New York: Rizzoli, 2011.

Time Magazine. "Art: More Than Modern." March 31, 1958.

Toshiko Mori Architect. New York: The Monacelli Press, 2008.

Watson-Irwin, Jane, Papers. New Canaan Historical Society Library.

Weber, Nicholas Fox. *The Bauhaus Group: Six Masters of Modernism*. New York: Alfred A. Knopf, 2009.

Wolf, Barbara. *Philip Johnson: Diary of an Eccentric Architect*. Film. New York: Checkerboard Film Foundation, Inc., 1996.

Credits

Every effort has been made to contact the copyright holders of photographs. Any errors or ommissions will be corrected in future editions.